all in the
Detail

all in the
Detail

over 400 finishing touches that make a house a home

Caroline Clifton-Mogg

RYLAND
PETERS
& SMALL
LONDON NEW YORK

SENIOR DESIGNER Toni Kay

SENIOR EDITOR Clare Double

PICTURE RESEARCH Emily Westlake

PRODUCTION MANAGER Patricia Harrington

ART DIRECTOR Leslie Harrington

PUBLISHING DIRECTOR Alison Starling

First published in the UK in 2009
This edition published in 2011
by Ryland Peters & Small
20–21 Jockey's Fields
London WC1R 4BW
www.rylandpeters.com

10 9 8 7 6 5 4 3 2

ISBN: 978-1-84975-133-9

A CIP record for this book is available
from the British Library.

PRINTED IN CHINA

contents

introduction

'God is in the detail' Mies van der Rohe supposedly said, and although he was more likely to have been talking, in one sense at least, about the importance of making sure that every last light switch and door handle was the right one for a particular space, I think he also meant that, when you decorate and furnish a home or even a single room, it is important to spend time getting every aspect, even the smallest, right – it's the couture dress worn with laddered tights syndrome (the insignificant laddered tights will give you far more anguish than the memorable dress gives you pleasure). So I think the message is that, if you pay attention to the details, the larger issues will, by and large, fall into place.

When you move into somewhere new there are a lot of initial, large decisions to be made, some of them more interesting than others, but all of them important. Sensibly, we tend to devote a lot of time to planning the kitchen, for example, and choosing the right units and equipment. You might research sofas, chairs and tables, test out beds and look at bath and shower designs. All this is very important – these are the big, expensive decisions that it is vital to get right. But when you've made those choices and done – as you see it – the hard work, with the walls painted in flattering shades, the kitchen up and running, the furniture in place and the curtains and blinds hung, you might well sense that there is something intangible missing, and that is because the finishing touches – the details that make a space into a home – are not yet in place.

This book, it is important to say, is not primarily about architectural details as such, although they are extremely important in the greater scheme of things. We are concentrating here on decorative detail; this is not at all the same thing as fussy detail, although it may sometimes be depicted as such – but not in this book!

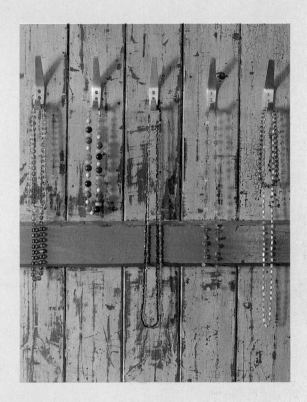

One dictionary definition of 'detail' is 'an item, a particular', and that is indeed what decorative details are. They are the items, the particular things that lift a room – the pictures, the mirrors, the books, the china and glass and the cushions; the seemingly unimportant extras that are actually, in many ways, the most important of all.

What we know, formally, as details are to many of us less formally and better known as 'stuff'. The 'stuff' we all have – our books, our china, our bits – are things that we sometimes hardly register as being there. These are our everyday possessions – things that are part of us, which may have been bought or been given, inherited or borrowed – but that are with us, wherever we go. How we use them and what we do with them is important because, in a way, they define us. We have all been to houses where 'stuff' is everywhere, lying around almost at random and looking definitely unloved; but in another house, the same things (sometimes almost literally) are arranged and displayed in such a way that lifts the spirits and makes you want to go home and rearrange your own possessions.

So, back home and surrounded by your stuff, your details, the task is to use them to personalize your surroundings, to give them an identity that is unique and which conveys to a visitor the impression of who you are, your taste and

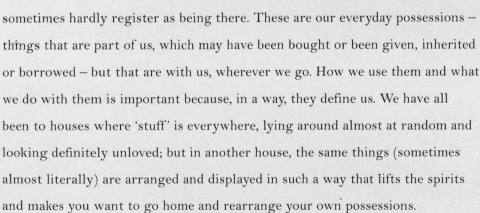

likes and dislikes. Our homes are defined by our possessions, whether we like it or not, and so are we ourselves defined; for make no mistake, when someone new comes into your home, the first things they notice are not the large semi-permanent pieces – the fitted kitchen, the new wet room. No, they notice the pictures and the way that they are hung, the decorative objects, the way the books are ranged on the shelves, and the flowers on the table. Those are the things by which you are, to some degree, judged – in decorative terms, at least.

For that reason alone, it would seem important to have the things that you love displayed to best advantage; without them, our living quarters have no personality, and might as well be a room set on a shop floor, or a show apartment in a new development. It is only when our books and photographs, pictures and cushions, are brought in and put in place that our houses and flats become real homes.

Luckily, all the thought that you put earlier into making the structural and design decisions means that, with luck, you now have the bones – the basic structure of the room – in place and are therefore ready to start applying the details, fleshing out the spaces and making your mark.

We often don't realize, until we think about it, just what we have around us and, more importantly, how what we have around us could look better. We are all, at heart, collectors; a collection, after all, can be as few as two – two flower-strewn jugs, two vintage photos; it is the way that they are displayed that brings them to life and, more importantly, brings to life the room they are in. These finishing touches are not shallow or unimportant – far from it – and in this book

we have tried to look at the value of the finishing touch, and how to make those touches count. We look at the principles of display and arrangement, of the importance of scale, and how to edit your possessions so that they make the most impact (sometimes it is more interesting to show only a few of a type of objects, rotating pieces over a period of time). There are tips on how to show and combine different pieces – different sorts of 'stuff' – to best effect; the importance of focal points in a room; and using colour to best effect.

We look, for example, in detail – as you might say – at the grouping and hanging of pictures and mirrors, which are always the first thing that people notice on entering a room, and we look also at the comfort-zone details – the cushions, sofa throws, lampshades, and of course flowers and plants – the soft pieces that make a room welcoming.

China and glass pop up throughout the book, for these are the original decorative details, designed for centuries as decorative objects in their own right, and important just for being themselves. These pieces deserve respect and to be displayed in ways that add to their charms, rather than detract from them. We also look at the wider definition of decorative objects and collections of objects, and how and where they may be put together to best effect, in which context we also look at the huge decorative potential of not only table surfaces but also the now sometimes redundant fireplace and mantelpiece – that often-neglected elephant in the room.

Details are what make domestic life pleasant and warm; for that reason alone, if for no other, it must be worth working on the details to make where you live truly worth living in!

pictures, mirrors
and other wall art

For many people, pictures and photographs are the first resources to be called on when it comes to adding individuality to a room. But a successful hang – as they call it in the art world – is actually much trickier than it might at first appear.

the art of placing pictures

Using space on a wall or walls to display pictures, whether they are powerful paintings, delicate watercolours, prints, drawings or sketches, is a skill, sometimes an art, and too often an art that is, sadly, unrecognized by others. Many people think that any fool can hang a picture – and of course in the practical sense they can – but to hang a picture or pictures well is a skill of quite a different order.

Too often a picture is hung in single, solitary isolation, to be joined later by a second one which, although sharing no visual connection with the first, is automatically hung in the remaining space on that piece of wall. This approach rarely, if ever, works – why should it? Every element of an interior decoration scheme

ABOVE LEFT: A collection of canine pictures of different shapes and sizes arranged in a pleasing, unusual group; in the centre, the frames of five of the pictures overlap a larger print.

LEFT: Although they seem to be placed informally against the wall, the arrangement of these three overlapping pictures is actually very carefully thought out.

OPPOSITE ABOVE LEFT: A handsome still life of vessels is hung above a group of actual objects that echo the theme of the painting.

OPPOSITE ABOVE RIGHT: In a blue-painted bedroom, plates and prints that echo the colour scheme are grouped together behind the bed.

A group of closely related pictures has been hung together on a white-painted brick wall, above a bench and a long table on which objects make a visual link to the wall.

should be designed to work in harmony and scale, and such basic design rules apply just as much to the pictures on the walls as the seating and lighting.

A blank wall should be seen as an exciting opportunity – an ideal background against which a pleasing composition can be arranged. Regard it as a canvas, perhaps, or, even better, like a display surface in a professional picture gallery, where the works are hung in the way that will display their charms to absolute best advantage.

Successful displays of wall art rely for their impact on a connecting factor, which might be the subject matter, the medium in which they are painted, their overall size or even the colour or shape of each frame. Once the common denominator has been established – not always easy, but there is always at least one link – the chosen pieces should be arranged as a single composition and hung with mathematical precision; this is usually achieved with a pencil, tape measure and a plumb line or a weight on the end of a piece of string.

OPPOSITE: This group of related botanical prints is grouped closely, very closely, together for maximum impact. They are also hung as low as is practicably possible, just above the bed head, the design of which echoes the botanical theme.

THIS PAGE: A set of four pictures, hung the length of a handsome wooden refectory table, becomes part of a composition that also includes pottery and plants.

The central canvas here is strong enough to stand alone, but it gains importance through being hung with two smaller canvases in similar tones, and in front of a table arrangement that again echoes its tones.

It is near impossible, unless you are blessed with a perfect eye, to hang a successful group of pictures directly onto a wall. Most people resort to a variation on the most basic, but foolproof, of methods: setting out all the pictures directly onto a flat surface (usually the floor) and moving their positions until they are happy with the arrangement and composition. A rough sketch or even mobile phone picture at this juncture will ensure that you can convert the idea into reality. The most important thing to get right is not so much the juxtaposition of images, but the spacing between different pictures and different frames. Too little space between each one and they will all look cramped; too much and each picture will appear to be floating in space. The width of frame makes a difference, as do the dimensions of each picture. Large images need far more space around them –

ABOVE: **At first glance this arrangement may seem random or haphazard, but all the pictures are connected – both as bright, colourful compositions and because they are hung in gilded frames of every shape and size.**

LEFT: A subtle, but carefully composed, group of objects and a single picture.

RIGHT: Ranged closely, these three pictures have a weight that they would not achieve if hung individually.

sometimes a whole wall – while small images look best designed as a group. The other important rule, and one that is broken all the time, is to have the base line of the group far enough down the wall. There is nothing more distressing to the eye than one or several pictures hung halfway up the wall and bearing no relation to the furniture or objects below. In all the photographs in this chapter, you will note that every image is hung in such a position that it ties in with what is below. A refinement of this is to include the images on the wall in an arrangement of objects on a surface below, forming a three-dimensional composition. If all this sounds too technical, be not alarmed: like so many written instructions for everyday tasks – how to boil an egg or sew a hem – the reality is far easier than the technicalities; your eye and instinct will always see you through.

OPPOSITE ABOVE: **A group of designer sketches hung in a block is made into a composition by association with a collection of glass that echoes the dominant colours.**

OPPOSITE BELOW: **Light, white and geometric; the group of graphic prints, all in white-painted frames, has been hung with mathematical precision to follow the lines of the white-painted bench and table below.**

THIS PAGE: **A double dose of a floral print – oversized on the wall, and reduced as a single cushion below. A pair of cushions would have been excessive.**

how to display photographs

A photograph has a personality and emotional pull that is very different to the more cerebral response most of us have to a picture. Perhaps it is because the image on view is one of past or present reality – events that happened, people who are living or have lived. Whatever the underlying reasons, it is true that photographs are viewed in a different way from traditional art; inspected more closely, every detail noted. This means successful photograph hanging is usually more intimate than that of other pictures. Often hung at eye level or below, photographs look good massed together, sometimes slightly overlapping, almost as if they are in a giant album.

+ Walls are not the only places where photographs can be displayed; shelves, tables, odd corners and, of course, the floor all make good homes for a collection.

+ If your photographs are displayed on a shelf or the floor, alter their positions from time to time so that different images are emphasized, and different stories told.

+ Generally speaking, display colour with colour, and black and white either on its own or with sepia-tinted prints, to get the best from an arrangement.

+ Many old photographs are relatively small and look good in oversized decorative or ornate frames that will draw attention to the image.

+ Look out for old watch cases; often made in metal or leather to hold half-hunter pocket watches, they are free-standing, and suit small photographs admirably.

In literature mirrors have often been endowed with magical qualities – the ability to speak or to show in the glass the answer to some searching question. In real life, too, they are just as magical, and can be used to great effect in every room.

the magic of mirrors

Modern mirror magic is not much to do with fairies, white rabbits or wicked stepmothers; instead, it is a visual magic – the way that a mirror can alter the size and proportions of a room, emphasize specific features, and bring light to obscure corners. In decorative terms, mirrors are essential; they give a depth and fluidity that is lacking in a room hung only with pictures.

There has always been a cachet to mirrors, from the very first examples, which were not glass but convex discs of bronze, tin or silver with highly polished surfaces. Glass with a metallic backing appeared in the 13th century; when it was first produced, it was naturally extremely expensive and could only be made in small

sizes. By the late 17th century, it was widely understood how important a part mirrored glass could play in interior decoration, and the frames began to be as important as the glass within – sometimes inlaid with ivory and elaborate veneers, or carved into fantastical garlands and wreaths, like those of the master carver,

OPPOSITE: Relatively easy to find, these bevelled mirrors, grouped together, look far better than if they were in assorted frames. There is a coherence to the group, and the variety of shapes makes a very pleasing composition.

BELOW LEFT: A dramatic frame is complemented by mirrored glass. It's all the more appropriate since it is hung against a very vibrant wallpaper, a design far too strong to display a picture to advantage.

The large mirror here, with its silvered wooden frame, is very much part of an overall decorative composition. There is no additional colour in the hall; the effect is achieved with shape and reflection.

LEFT: **A mirror in an imperfect or damaged frame can be given a new lease of life with a coat of paint. This large mirror is very effective above and beside the bath, emphasizing the shape of the bathtub and increasing the sense of space.**

OPPOSITE ABOVE LEFT: **In a small bedroom an oversized mirror, seemingly nonchalantly propped against the wall, makes the room feel larger as well as becoming an integral part of the decorative scheme.**

OPPOSITE ABOVE RIGHT: **Carefully positioned to reflect a large poster on the opposite wall, this mirror has two uses, both practical and decorative.**

OPPOSITE BELOW LEFT: **In what is almost a sleight of hand, two mirrors lean one against the other, giving interesting, and slightly disorientating, reflective images.**

OPPOSITE BELOW RIGHT: **A group of old bevelled mirrors is both striking and decorative in this light country bathroom.**

Grinling Gibbons. The fashion for overmantels, when mirrors were built into the chimneypiece as part of an architectural ensemble, was popularized by Robert Adam in the 18th century, and continued into the 19th.

Today we are freer with how and where we use our mirrors, but their placing is still vital. On entering a room, the eye is drawn first to a mirror, then to whatever else is on the walls, so care must be taken that the mirror does not work to disadvantage; importantly, what is reflected in the mirror should work with the other wall art. Mirrors which are too big to be hung with ease can be very effective on the floor, propped against the wall, where they act almost as a door to a reflected room beyond.

Mirrored furniture, very popular in the 1930s, is now being made again and desks, chests, consoles and tables can add a reflective note to bedrooms, bathrooms and living rooms. The variety of glass finishes, available both in framed mirrors and furniture designs, ranges from smoked and bronzed to various antique finishes, which give a soft muted tone to the glass, gentler than a modern finish.

OPPOSITE: **In a clever trompe l'oeil joke, this wall is hung with wallpaper printed with a picture of an actual library; books do paper a room.**

ABOVE RIGHT: **A collection of postcards, trinkets and ephemera is displayed in what appears to be a random manner, but which is, in fact, extremely disciplined.**

BELOW RIGHT AND FAR RIGHT: **The beauty and romance of a map is hard to appreciate in folded form. Here, an old map has been carefully framed in sections and hung so that it covers an entire wall, where it can be studied in all its intricate detail.**

BOTTOM RIGHT: **A beautiful textile always looks good as a hanging. This embroidered silk, exactly the width of the seat below, is no exception.**

Think laterally when it comes to adorning the walls. Many objects, from hats to kitchen utensils, look even better attached to the wall rather than being hidden in drawers or cupboards.

other wall art

The reason that we like to hang things on walls is to give personality to a space. A room with nothing on the walls is always slightly dead – think of the way a room alters when you have taken down the pictures prior to moving out. What goes on the wall need not be confined to the obvious; pictures and photographs are always interesting, but plenty of other categories of things, many of which were not originally designed for display, can light up both a wall and a room. Maps and charts come into this category, as do many textiles, ceramics and ephemera. From patchwork quilts, shawls or a length of interesting fabric, to postcards and bas-relief plaster forms, plates and dishes, think what would give you pleasure to see, then arrange it into a harmonious composition, taking the other elements of the room into consideration.

flowers
and plants

OPPOSITE ABOVE LEFT:
An antique lustreware sugar bowl, placed against a background of rosy wallpaper, holds heads of overblown anemones that continue the pink theme and suit the mood of nostalgia.

OPPOSITE ABOVE RIGHT:
Three different shapes and sizes of the same vase are grouped tightly together and filled with heads of the same close-cut blooms.

OPPOSITE BELOW LEFT:
An informal group of flowers, berries and twigs, in a small white-glazed bowl.

OPPOSITE BELOW RIGHT:
Mixed summer roses are grouped together in an antique teapot that matches their old-fashioned charm.

A single striking branch in a clear glass vase, part of a larger arrangement of objets trouvés, makes its own pattern against the wall.

Of all the details that you might want to have in a room, flowers are the most obvious. Everyone loves flowers; they're beautiful and they're natural, and whether they are formally arranged or informally, they can make a room come instantly alive.

bunches and posies

We are, apparently, buying more flowers than ever, a fact that can only bring pleasure to all. A room without flowers seems unlived in and uncared for – even the humblest bunch of spring daffodils lights up a table or a corner far more effectively than a 100-watt bulb. As well as being important details, flowers are part of the decoration of a room and, just as with other aspects of interior decoration, the flowers we choose and the way we like to see them displayed are subject to changing fashions and contemporary taste. Few of us now would like to fill our rooms with huge Victorian floral displays, as elaborate as the ballgowns of the same period; and although there is still a place for structured, traditional arrangements, they tend to be used mostly on equally

The delicate petals and scent of sweet peas need to be appreciated at close quarters, as in this narrow-necked glass vase.

ABOVE: **No bloom is too small to make an impression when it is displayed in all its miniature perfection.**

ABOVE RIGHT: **These double sweet peas, with stems cut short, flow over the sides of the contrasting lime-green glass vase.**

RIGHT: **The stems of this large-flowered shrub have been cut right back to give an impression of overflowing abundance.**

OPPOSITE: **Lilac flowers, which grow on long arching stems, have been cut right back and loosely arranged in a large glazed pottery jug; the effect is informal and very pleasing.**

traditional, formal occasions such as weddings. No, the buzz word of the moment is 'natural' – natural in the varieties of flower that we favour, and in the way they are arranged; we seem to prefer simpler, straight-from-the-garden arrangements (although such simplicity is often the result of much skill) that emphasize the flowers' natural beauty. These might be long-stemmed herbaceous blooms arranged with artful casualness in tall containers or, at the other end of the spectrum, tightly wound posies and bunches, often a single variety and colour, arranged in a dome shape with short stems.

Whether the bunches are tall or tiny, it is important to get the scale and balance right. Certain proportions work – low arrangements should be a little wider than the container and about half the height of the vase; tall-stemmed flowers should ideally be about one and a half to two times taller than the vase or container they are in.

RIGHT: Although everything is so simple, this is still an unexpected arrangement of yellow gladioli, arranged in six different jugs, carefully placed by a mirror and on the floor.

BELOW: Single, beautiful anemone blooms are given their own delicate gilded teacup in which to shine.

OPPOSITE LEFT: There is something remarkably appropriate in these traditional yellow roses being bunched tightly together in a traditional painted vase dating from the 19th century.

OPPOSITE RIGHT: A composition of colour, with the heads of purple iris displayed in a glass in front of deeper-hued hyacinth bulbs.

When choosing flowers for display, group small flowers together rather than mixing them with larger blooms, where they will be lost in the crowd. Instead, emphasize their miniature appeal by arranging them in small containers, placed on low surfaces where you can look down on them and admire them close to. Conversely, tall flowers work best at eye level, where their structure and form can be appreciated. As with many other decorative details, flowers usually make more impact when massed together, but that doesn't mean to say that they should always be put into the same container; a bunch can look very effective divided between several small vases or other vessels. This is one reason for thinking laterally about containers in general; there is a world beyond conventional vases, and a stock of old tumblers and jars in different sizes are useful as liners for less waterproof holders.

Don't reserve flowers solely for the main reception rooms – yes, they are always lovely in the living room, but flowers in the kitchen brighten any chores, in the bedroom they make you smile, and in the bathroom they give an instant air of sybaritic luxury. You don't need many and they don't have to be expensive; it is better to buy several bunches of cheap seasonal flowers rather than one or two of the most expensive hothouse blooms.

Whether out of economic necessity or aesthetic choice, many people love the idea of single blooms; it is a contemporary look achieved with little effort or outlay.

single stems and blooms

The complexity of a flower – the shape and shades of a petal, the line of a stem, the tone of a leaf – means that often, although we appreciate the whole, we sometimes overlook the beauty of the particular. Displaying a flower or stem in a single holder is a way of appreciating it both from an aesthetic point of view and a botanical one. A lone flower is a dramatic gesture, and both tall and miniature blooms can benefit from the single-minded treatment. It is the perfect way to give a new life to a flower whose stem has broken short, or the last bloom from a larger bunch, and here you can take time to match the perfect bloom to the perfect container.

ABOVE: The perfect rose is a horticultural ideal and this lovely bloom looks its very best in a small rose vase that does not try to compete with the beauty of the most perfect of all flowers.

LEFT: Alone in a crowd – a great way to display flowers that might be too small for a larger display or which have short or broken stems. Some are displayed in a specially designed holder and others in small bottles. Massed together, they make a pleasing group.

OPPOSITE LEFT: An interesting group – two single stems, each in very different containers, linked by colour and unusual form.

OPPOSITE RIGHT: One of the pleasures of displaying single blooms is matching the flower to precisely the right vase. Anemones have a peculiarly late 19th-century quality, so this pairing, with a painted panelled vase, is a match made in floral heaven.

There is something both fresh and refreshing about using flowering (or even non-flowering) plants in the same decorative way that you would use cut flowers.

planted arrangements

Our attitude towards indoor plants has changed; dark, large-leafed aspidistras and Swiss cheese plants are out, and we tend towards softer shapes and tones of green, such as ornamental grasses and jasmine, as well as plants that flower inside. Forced bulbs – scented hyacinths and paper-white narcissi, plus daffodils of all kinds, tulips, crocuses and the tiny grape hyacinth – can be charming, adding life and warmth to any room. Unforced plants such as wood violets, violas and pansies, in fact almost all plants that look good in window boxes, will suit a pretty container. Small flowering plants will grace a dining table, at each place or marching enfilade down the centre; put them in miniature terracotta pots or small pails, or try clear or coloured glasses – earth or moss seen through the glass looks suitably rustic.

ABOVE: **Tiny viola plants, the most delicate and charming of woodland flowers, are planted in a heavy metal pot where their fragile beauty is accentuated.**

BELOW: **Miniature roses look best in a container that contrasts in texture with their colour and delicate form. A silver bowl gives just the right amount of hard-edged luxury.**

OPPOSITE: **Two is company, five a party. Pots of golden narcissi, decanted into simple metal containers, bring spring into the house.**

ABOVE: **A fragile orchid is seen to striking advantage planted in a container that has been wrapped in a seriously rustic woven bag.**

unusual vases

One of the great pleasures of bringing flowers into the house is to show them in ways that make them real decorative details – displays that people notice and admire, and that bring definition and interest to other aspects of the room. As flower arrangements become less formal, so many more sorts of containers can be transformed into unusual vases.

Almost anything can make a great container for flowers; some of the most attractive, like baskets and boxes, will not of course be waterproof and will need liners, which could be anything from a jam jar to a tin can. Keep old tumblers and fancy condiment jars so that you have a store of different shapes and sizes to choose from.

As far as deciding what to use as a container, go through the cupboards – not only the china cupboard, but also in the kitchen and the bedroom and bathroom. There will be obvious ceramic

candidates – mugs and cups (from small coffee to large tea) and jugs of all sizes, but the fun starts when you extend the remit. Look at different-sized bowls, from soup to salad; coffee- and teapots; soup tureens; sauce boats and sugar bowls; eggcups; and brandy and liqueur glasses (these last work very well with broken-stemmed flowers and small blooms).

Then there are tins, buckets, bottles and boxes. The most successful pairings are often the most contrary – hothouse roses in a zinc bucket do the trick, and branches of lilac from the garden look wonderful in a 19th-century hand-painted art vase. Look for contrasts of colour and texture and experiment – it's the easiest way to get new ideas.

✦ Once you get into the way of thinking about alternative containers, thrift shops and second-hand sales can take on a whole new meaning; look out particularly for larger containers and galvanized buckets and pitchers.

✦ Although water-retaining floral foam is now widely used, traditional flower-arranging aids include chicken wire scrunched into a ball, and glass flower-arranging frogs – small glass domes with holes, which come in different shapes and sizes and sit on the floor of the vase. Particularly pretty in clear vases, glass frogs can still be found occasionally in antique shops and on auction sites, and have a unique charm.

✦ Always use clean vases and containers and cut off any leaves that might be under water. Packets of flower food really do help to prolong the life of cut flowers.

soft
furnishings

Comfortable large cushions placed in the corners of sofas and chairs always look inviting; cushions like these should be plumped up, rather than being beaten into severe submission.

LEFT: **A group of small cushions, rectangular and square, in a variety of designs but all within the same colour palette. The tassels at the corners of the striped cushions are an effective detail.**

ABOVE: **A group of very different cushion designs works because the combined colour palette is both subtle and neutral.**

BELOW: **A humble plaid blanket has been elevated into a piece of decorative design with vivid-coloured velvet lining and edging.**

Change the cushions and you change the room; add to the mixture an unusual throw or two, and almost any room is immediately made both more interesting and more comfortable.

cushions and throws

As every decorator worth his trimmings knows, one of the easiest ways of adding quick and striking detail to a room is to sharpen up the soft furnishings – the chairs and sofas. The easiest way to do that is not to replace the covers – always expensive and sometimes unnecessary – but to think about adding cushions and throws. These last are a new, and seemingly permanent, addition to the repertoire of decorative detail. This really is instant decorating – immediately brightening up the space and sometimes completely changing the look of the whole room. Even though it is instant, spare a little time to think about exactly what is required. For instance, although one might say that a single cushion, unless it is particularly striking, is usually not enough, it is also important to avoid overcrowding a sofa or chair. There is a point when too many cushions merely look unapproachable rather

than inviting; there should be just enough to fill the space comfortably, whether that means one or ten.

Then there is the question of shape and colour. Nothing looks duller (think sofa showroom) than a row of identical cushions; as with pictures, a certain variety is essential. However, remember balance and scale; if cushions are to be arranged next to each other, they should relate – some rectangular, some square perhaps, one pair larger, one smaller, but, when used together, making a pleasing and harmonious design.

The question of throws – what to choose and how to arrange it – is not quite as easy as first it may seem. Any old spare blanket draped over a chair that is on its last legs is hardly a decorative detail, and that is the point. A throw, as well as having practical possibilities, should also be decorative and work with the rest of the scheme of the room, enhancing the space and making it feel more comfortable and attractive. The choice is huge, from an antique shawl to a contemporary hand-knit or a plaid rug; throws are an ideal way to show off a beautiful textile that is too small or too unusual to use anywhere else, and a contrast in texture will work well as long as there is some balance between the weight of the chair cover and the chosen throw.

ABOVE LEFT: Small cushions, rectangular and cylindrical, are grouped together on an antique wooden bench. Many are made from old textiles.

LEFT: A Victorian button-back chair has both cushions and a related throw in a contemporary design, using a neutral palette of colours.

OPPOSITE ABOVE LEFT: A riot of texture! On a leather seat, coloured fur is used as a throw, with a bold sequinned cushion on top. The result is both amusing and inviting.

OPPOSITE ABOVE RIGHT: A clever use of colour and pattern: an oriental, brightly patterned and coloured wrap is used as a throw over a 20th-century chair, which is upholstered in grey wool.

OPPOSITE BELOW: In this space of otherwise sober and neutral design, cushions add accents of colour and pattern that lift the whole room.

adding colour and pattern

Cushions are small objects within the context of a room, so it is easy to experiment with colour and pattern, try out new ideas and change things around relatively frequently. Think of cushions and throws as interior fashion – pieces that are brought in to match a mood and a moment. They really are the way to change a room – and nearly always for the better. This is absolutely the place to use pieces of vintage or antique fabrics that seem too small to be otherwise displayed; made into a cushion cover, or even used as a panel in a larger cushion, their original quality shines through. Whatever pattern or colour you choose, scale and proportion, as always, are important; a small cushion on a large sofa never works, and is even more inappropriate when its bright colour or pattern is lost against an oversized, monochrome background.

+ Colour used as an accent is a vital part of an interior decoration scheme. Brightly coloured cushions can fill this role, with shots of sharp or bright colours that might be overbearing in a more dominant position bringing the overall scheme into focus.

+ That said, remember to take into account the theme of the room; the sofa cushions must, in a visual way, tie in with the other elements of the room.

+ Battered and stained cushion covers simply will not do. A stop-gap solution is to sew a decorative front or panel onto an existing cushion cover, or use remnants as bolster ends or as trims along seat covers.

+ Fabric remnants reduced in price in the sales can be a useful source of bits that may come in useful, decoratively, in the future. Buy them when you see them, and store them.

Historically, bed linen was always a treasured and valued part of the household furnishings, listed on inventories and bequeathed to favoured members of the family. Often beautifully decorated, such linens were still essentially practical items.

bed linen

Today, although bed linen is still of course a practical essential, it is also an important element in a bedroom scheme – a decorative detail that actually carries as much weight as the colour of the walls or floor. We now buy matching sets of sheets and pillowcases as a matter of course, rather than using whatever is to hand, and new sets are chosen to work with the colours and style of the room. Like cushions and lampshades, the variety and choice available means that a new set of linen or a new bedspread or duvet cover can, at a

stroke, transform the look of a room, so it is worth giving thought to the design or designs that you choose.

Most importantly, the bed linen should work with the bed, and colour and pattern should be used judiciously. Fashions change: in the 1960s the last word in bed linen fashion was bright colours, often teamed with chocolate brown or navy blue; then came pattern, with sheets that either looked like cottage garden borders or pop-art paintings. Today, things have calmed down – which, since the bedroom is supposed to be a haven of

ABOVE LEFT: The cut-work cover on this bed is an integral part of the decorative scheme; its relative brightness stops the room from becoming a study in brown.

TOP: A beautiful antique Gothic bed head is enhanced by a padded bolster covered in a delicate flower pattern that echoes the wall colour.

ABOVE: This canopied bed has curtains in a faded flower design that echoes, but does not compete with, the stronger flowers at the window.

OPPOSITE: An immensely comfortable contemporary bed, with a deeply padded and buttoned wraparound bed head and bed linen in soothing tones of taupe.

THIS PAGE AND OPPOSITE LEFT:
A charming, serene room in which every
detail has been carefully thought out.
It has a pale painted floor, antique iron
bedstead and painted wooden fold-up
tables; in contrast are touches of colour
in the embroidered sheet and duvet cover,
the quilt and the sharp citrus design tied
onto the bed head.

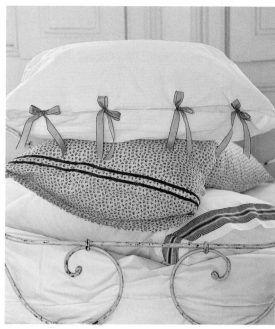

LEFT: **A selection of pretty pillows, some of them ornamental: one tied with ribbons instead of buttons, and two trimmed with ribbon and braid.**

BELOW: **An unashamedly vintage bedroom: the faded roses of the 19th-century wallpaper are echoed in the quilt as well as the pillows.**

calm relaxation, is no bad thing – and muted colour or colours tend to work better, whether your bed and room are antique or contemporary in style. It is certainly not necessary to have only one design for sheet, duvet and pillows – and certainly not for any cover or quilt. As with the decoration of other rooms, a pleasing design can be one that combines several different shades and/or patterns, but all chosen to work together within a palette of colour or pattern, with perhaps extra cushions to add a sharp accent or counterpoint to the rest of the scheme.

Comfort is also important – some might say that it is *the* most important element in a room in which you spend so much time. Pillows, of which there should be enough to be able to read comfortably in bed, should be the best quality that you can afford (and replaced when they become lumpy), and blankets or duvet covers should be light and warm – again, the more you invest, the better the result. The trend towards having a throw or blanket at the end of the bed is an extra opportunity to add not only warmth but a touch of decoration and even luxury to the scheme.

For many people, the only possible bedroom option is to choose a colour – any colour – just as long as it is white; nothing else will fit the bedroom bill.

the all-white bed

Historically, white was the only colour available for bed linen. There was no choice, and for many traditionalists today that remains the case. White is the colour and that is all there is to it. If that is your view, the good news is that almost any look, from sparkling modern to nostalgic vintage, can be found in white. The bad news is that an all-white room can look clinical, boring even, if there is not some variety within the different elements, particularly on the actual bed itself. White can be so many things – so many tones and shades – that the answer, as so often in decoration, is to vary the textures as well as the tones; mix materials – soft wool, smooth and quilted cotton, textured linen. Add embroidery, fringing and braid, as well as fine lines of contrast colour; mix it all up and you will have a bedroom of subtle charm.

ABOVE: In an all-white room, interest is maintained by a diversity of shape and texture and the slightest smattering of roses on the pillows.

LEFT: Old, embroidered strips are made into pretty pillows that, massed together, add charm to a bed.

RIGHT: A handsome brass bed is dressed with white, including the reading lamps; a heavily fringed, traditional bedspread adds warmth.

In an attic, an all-white room, designed to maximize the space, could be cold, with its painted floor, furniture and neutral wallpaper; but it is made to feel luxurious with the addition of a heavily quilted white bedspread, luxuriously layered over the end of the antique, painted French wooden bed.

finishing touches for guest rooms

If it's all in the detail, then the detail certainly comes into play when you are looking after others at home. Overnight guests are the ultimate challenge to a hostess: how can you make their stay with you both memorable and comfortable? The answer is, naturally, in the detail: an old maxim from all those 'How to be a Good Hostess' books recommended that the said hostess slept a night in every one of her spare rooms. This you may not want to do – indeed, you may not have more than one guest room; but at least go into the room and look at it clinically from a stranger's point of view. Lovely bed linen; a light that is tall enough to illuminate your book, plus, of course, a good book to read; a small vase of freshly picked flowers and a glass for midnight water; and – important this – a bedside alarm clock: all these are the considerate finishing touches.

- ✦ Bedside table lamps must be at least as tall as the bed head; it is astonishing how often a table lamp the size of a squashed mushroom is thought to be sufficient light by which to read. A more permanent, but also fail-safe, option is a wall-hung swivel and adjustable reading lamp.

- ✦ On the book front, a current magazine, a book of carefully sourced anecdotes, and the latest must-read biography would make the perfect guest library.

- ✦ A comfortable, small upholstered chair is an absolute luxury in a guest room; they may not use it, but the idea of private relaxation will be so appealing to your guests.

- ✦ Traditionally, the tin of biscuits, tea-making facilities and added bathroom bonuses – toothpaste, bath oil and any extra unguents – were always welcome in a guest bedroom and bathroom. Any of the above will always be much appreciated by your guests.

china and
glass

A well-set table is the ultimate detail. It says far more than an arrangement of china and glass; it is an invitation to enjoy yourself, to relax and have fun. That is why, no matter what the occasion, every table should be set with care.

table settings

ABOVE: **Unusual tableware like this salt cellar includes the sort of objects that add interest and amusement to a table.**

Tables have been used to impress for hundreds of years. From the lavish display of valuable plate on the side to the costly glass, silver and porcelain on the table, the dining table was the place to tell those who entered your house the extent of your power and wealth. Now, although a little bit of impressing may go on on the side, the idea of a well-laid table is to make your guests feel welcome. This you do by making an effort to decorate the table in an attractive way, choosing interesting china and glass and adding flowers, candles and other ornamental pleasures.

Now that meals seldom take place in a dedicated dining room, but in the kitchen or living room perhaps, even more emphasis should be placed on how the table is presented. There are as many ways to set a table as there are patterns of china and glass; contemporary or traditional, formal or informal, romantic or steely chic – it all depends on what we like, but also on what we own.

Table setting is in many ways a miniature form of interior decoration, but luckily one at which any amateur

A simple setting, but one that exudes prettiness; from the soft shades of pale grey and white to the cut-down peony blooms in a wine goblet, the picture is one of subtle style.

ABOVE: **An embroidered napkin is arranged in a floral swirl inside this delicate, hand-painted porcelain teacup and saucer.**

OPPOSITE RIGHT: **A festive answer to keeping cutlery in order: on a brightly patterned tablecloth, clusters of knives, forks and spoons are tied with cheerful bows of many different-patterned ribbons.**

TOP: **Ready for a party. Among the piles of plates, chunky knives and spoons are stacked in specially designed glazed holders.**

ABOVE RIGHT: **A heavy flat pebble that matches the texture of the unbleached linen napkin is used partly as decoration and partly for function, anchoring the napkin to its place setting.**

can excel; like grouped tablescapes (see page 138), setting a table in one style or another is a way of using what you have in a new and inventive way. Most of us have more than one pattern of china and glass, albeit not an entire service. Sometimes we are surprised by how much we actually own, when we start looking in the cupboards, which works well with the idea that a table set with just one service is a slightly old-fashioned one. Today it's likely that you might combine one pattern of china for the main plates with another for side plates, which picks up one of the dominant colours in the first service, and then perhaps something entirely different for the last course. If, however, you do only have one set of china, the look can be just as easily changed

with different cloths and mats. In any case, table level is where you should start. This is the canvas; build up from here, adding colour and texture as you go.

One (light-hearted) way to think of it is as a production, with the table as the stage, the table settings the set, as well as the props, and the diners the actors. This way you can think beyond the actual surface of the table into the wider landscape – the room itself, the surrounding walls, the overall lighting and the colours. Sometimes more is needed – a mirror, perhaps a picture, more lights. Think of texture and colour and pattern, of course, and try to do something unusual. Some like the table crowded, some prefer it with more space to move around. Alternative thinking is good – using a bit of imagination to take what is there and extend it beyond what you might imagine. In one sense every meal and every table is a celebration, whether of the everyday or of the particular and unique. Time and trouble are the watchwords – not the amount of money spent, but the care taken.

LEFT AND OPPOSITE ABOVE LEFT: **Although this table setting is extremely simple, it is both attractive and inviting; nothing could be simpler. A runner in the centre of the table is linen, printed with wild roses and teamed with napkins that do not match but are edged in the same tones of red. White plates, pots of tulips in a square urn and glasses filled with rosé wine – a perfect combination.**

OPPOSITE ABOVE RIGHT: **East meets West in a black and white setting – black plates, white bowl, a deep red napkin, all tied together by the cheery polka-dot chopsticks.**

OPPOSITE BELOW LEFT: **A stylish way of serving condiments, in this case different types of sugar, but for salt, pepper and other necessary asides, a deep-sided tray with separate compartments within also fits the bill.**

OPPOSITE BELOW RIGHT: **All the pieces here fit into the same broad colour scheme of rose-pink, green and white. Stacked together they make a harmonious grouping, even before they are set out on the table.**

A large collection of tall glass candlesticks, few
of them matching, almost fills the dining table.
The candles themselves, in different shades of red,
pink and ivory, are an integral part of the overall look.

RIGHT: On a windowsill, in front of a white blind, is a group of simple, matching candlesticks, displayed closely together. They are arranged as much for effect as for function.

FAR RIGHT: These two ornate, carved wooden candlesticks, one with an old-fashioned candle spike, do not match but nevertheless work together as a pair.

Lighting is as important at the table as it is everywhere else in the house, and first and foremost it should flatter. No dinner will be enjoyed by a lady who sits with unforgiving lighting trained upon her.

candlesticks

Even after the newly invented electric light became ubiquitous for domestic lighting, candlelight remained – and is today – popular throughout the house, and almost essential at the dining table. Candles have always been an indicator of wealth, or the lack of it – rush lights and tallow (a wax derived from cattle and sheep suet, with an acrid smell) were the only candles available for most of the population; the rich had beeswax, which was pleasantly scented, but extremely expensive, and was therefore often kept for important occasions. Rare were the houses such as the Palace of Versailles, constructed in the 17th century by Louis XIV, where, in the Galerie des Glaces, 3000 candles were lit on a regular basis, their soft light reflected by over 350 mirrors hung the length of both sides of the long gallery.

Today, we have rediscovered candlelight and all its magical properties: at the dining table, where candles are now widely used, not only does the light work wonders for every complexion, but the flickering light adds an air of mystery and pleasure – excellent dining

An elaborate candelabrum sitting on a bathroom chair is ready to make bathtime all the more pleasant.

companions, both. Every other room, too, can benefit from the added richness and depth that candlelight gives to a space.

The range of candlesticks available, both new and antique, is vast. Most designs were originally made in pairs, but single candlesticks look just as effective, particularly when they are grouped in different sizes and shapes. Many collections have been formed from single sticks, sometimes of one material – glass, silver or ceramic – of one colour, or one shape. Display candlesticks beyond the dining table – on the mantelpiece, obviously, but perhaps grouped together rather than arranged symmetrically; on a side table, with a collection of other objects; or on a deep windowsill. Although white and ivory are the conventional colour choices for candles, it is amusing to use coloured candles occasionally, but keep the colours bold and confident and use them en masse, rather than in solitary or dual splendour.

A small group of mercury glass candlesticks has been arranged on a high shelf purely as decoration; candlesticks arranged like this always look better with candles ready to be lit.

BELOW: **Several metallic candlesticks, clustered closely together in an alcove, in front of a beaded blind.**

OPPOSITE ABOVE LEFT: **A pair of pressed-glass candelabra, with glass drops on chains, is arranged on a mantelpiece in front of a mirror that will reflect the light when they are lit.**

OPPOSITE ABOVE RIGHT: Once a familiar sight in every home, metal candle holders with handles to light the way to bed. These coloured enamel ones are still used.

OPPOSITE BELOW: **Just a collection of coloured glass candlesticks with not a matching pair between them, but what a cheerful sight.**

As part of a larger arrangement, shelves of glass goblets, candlesticks and carafes are interspersed with flowers, shells and decorative objects.

It is little wonder that glass has long been considered a thing of wonder – opaque or translucent, tough or fragile, coloured or clear, it can be blown into an airy decorative piece, gilded and painted, or moulded into a simple yet beautiful design.

glassware

Glass has been made for thousands of years. Not only did the Egyptians, Greeks and Romans make everyday glass – dishes, tumblers, goblets, bowls and cups – but we know from the examples that survive that they could make pieces of the most beautiful quality, design and decoration. These sophisticated techniques were lost for hundreds of years, and not seen again until Venetian glassmakers in the 14th century began to produce glass that once again went beyond the basic and functional.

There is something about glass, perhaps its contrary virtues of toughness and fragility, that makes designers

and craftsmen want to experiment and produce ever more beautiful pieces. It is also why many people feel that glass should, whenever possible, be displayed rather than hidden away. Why hide old decanters, for example, with collared and curved necks and bodies, decorated with cutting or faceted or moulded panels,

OPPOSITE ABOVE LEFT:
Blue-red glass, usually known as cranberry, is one of the original glass colours and varies in tone from almost blush pink to deep red. Different shapes and styles representing different periods work well as a group.

OPPOSITE ABOVE RIGHT:
Semi-opaque milky glass is one of the most attractive of glass tones and lends itself well to other colours and textures. On a tray, a collection of carafes and containers works well with sprigs of leaves.

OPPOSITE BELOW RIGHT:
Cut glass has a particular beauty all its own; the rich faceted surfaces of glasses and decanters were designed to sparkle in candlelight.

ABOVE: A moulded glass cake stand has been pressed into service as a delicate bowl for an assortment of shells and pebbles.

Pressed glass was produced in many different designs and styles, and looks particularly effective when used in profusion on a cut white cloth that emphasizes the nature of the glass.

Simple and effective: a shelf above the bed is lined with a collection of narrow-necked flasks, clear glass interposed with coloured examples of every shape and size.

on a top shelf? The variety of glass is so surprising and so extensive – coloured glass, for example, ranges from the traditional tones of cranberry, deep blue and green to the almost infinite paintbox of colours that became available when mass production of glass began in the 19th century. There is also glass where the surface has been cut or etched, engraved or moulded – all these techniques are fascinating and beautiful to live with.

Because glass is so varied and personal, it adds much to the decoration of a room, whether shown in single glory or massed perfection, and it mixes well with other materials, its translucent qualities adding to the pieces around it. It is easy to collect, too – examples of nearly every form of decoration and technique can be found, both new and old, some cheaply, some a little more expensive, in countless shops and stalls.

TOP: Luscious, coloured pressed glass, combined with exuberant green leaves – a simple way to show off unusual and charming shapes.

ABOVE: In a modern take on the Victorian glass dome with collections beneath, this glass urn has been used to display fragile and delicate shells.

Modern coloured glass, much
of it bought inexpensively, is
well served by being displayed
on glass shelves with lots of air
around each piece.

From the very beginning – which in ceramic terms was in China, over 2000 years ago – makers of ceramic wares, whether they were working with delicate porcelain or sturdier, everyday earthenware or stoneware, have always felt the need to design and make decorative pieces as well as functional ones.

ceramics

Whether it is a functional object or an item created for its decorative charms, we all have some ceramics in our homes. Because they are so ever-present, we often view them with an eye dulled by familiarity – an eye that does not see the potential that such pieces might have to play in the broader decorative sense. These pieces should be valued for their intrinsic beauty as well as for any functional charm that they have. A bit of cross-thinking might be required, and an instructive exercise might be to take such items out of their comfort zone, and look at them afresh as you would pictures or other ornaments; indeed, as with pictures, put them all on the floor and move them around, seeing what might work with what, and where. Think where else around the house they could be displayed, or used – could that pretty sugar bowl, for example, be used in the bathroom

TOP LEFT: The decorative charms of this fishy sauce boat are accentuated by the pile of white fish plates, which make a frame.

ABOVE LEFT: Displayed as art objects, three ceramic pieces are framed in a deep window and bathed in natural light.

ABOVE: A white ceramic soup tureen is the centre of a small decorative group including a glass decanter, creamware salt and pepper shakers and a delicate cut-work cloth.

OPPOSITE: Storing this large collection of flower holders in a glassed cupboard makes as much of a display as when the vases are in use.

for cotton wool or miniature soaps? Could that jug be used as a pen holder or for wooden spoons?

There are some obvious candidates. A fat, rounded soup tureen without its lid is a fine container for pots of flowering bulbs, or indoor climbers such as scented jasmine. Jugs make good flower holders, and old, single cups, particularly ornate, gilded examples, are appreciated as part of a small tablescape with other decorative objects, as too are little teapots or ornamental bowls. Plates and dishes can be hung on the wall, singly or in a group, or fixed upright on shelves between books, or other items in the same colours or shapes. It is just a question of looking afresh at old friends.

ABOVE: **Handmade ceramics are carefully shown off in a custom-made set of shelves.**

ABOVE LEFT: **A charming collection of antique novelty teapots, each in the shape of a vegetable; no further embellishment is required.**

CENTRE LEFT: **Instead of a deep bowl, a sprig-patterned, shallow soup dish is the perfect shape to hold fruit.**

BELOW LEFT: **Everyday bowls, but nevertheless displayed in decorative fashion, stacked in pleasing combinations.**

A ceramic cornucopia – from the overflowing shelves of the Welsh dresser to the urn and jug on the windowsill, this room is a celebration of all things ceramic. Although everything on the dresser shelves is functional, the pieces have been arranged in a manner that shows each jug and cup, plate and dish at its best.

No other room is more crammed with more decorative detail – or potential decorative detail – than the kitchen. This space, the heart of the home, is one that responds well to subtle additions.

kitchenware

Traditionally, kitchens in the country were the heart of the home – often the only really warm room – while urban kitchens were not as inviting. In the 20th century, kitchens were more often functional than friendly. Over the last few years the kitchen has evolved, and is still evolving, into something not only different, but definitely better. It all has much to do, of course, with the gradual disappearance of the dining room from our homes. The subsequent change in the role of the kitchen to accommodate not just cooking, but dining, living and entertaining means that more and more of us eat in the kitchen or very near to it, so we now need the room to be both accommodating and friendly, efficient but also attractive, functional but also decorated with style.

Now it is to be a room where personal style and decorative details count as much as in any other room. Luckily, all or many of the components are there in the room itself; it is just a question of identifying them, for it

ABOVE LEFT: **A traditional wooden plate rack acts as a textural display cabinet, with wooden dishes kept permanently between its bars.**

LEFT: **A narrow space has been fitted with shelves deep enough to hold a collection of old cake and compote stands. Traditional metal-topped glass canisters make a contrasting pattern below.**

RIGHT: **A modern kitchen area, part of a larger space, but arranged in traditional terms; the deep open storage unit defines the eating and cooking space and gives it warmth. Essential kitchenware is arranged in groups, almost like sculptural objects.**

is these objects, which can be found in many kitchens, that add definition and distinction to the room.

Displays of china and glass are one obvious answer; pleasing pieces of both everyday and special china have traditionally been shown off on the kitchen dresser or on open shelves. This is not the same as saying that everything you own should be on show – the mundane will not be improved by being on view, and should remain safely behind closed doors. It is the interesting and the attractive that should be out, perhaps a mixture of old and new, plain and patterned, arranged in a way that is both good-looking and close to hand.

Collections of kitchen necessities too, such as jugs or mixing bowls, can be attractive in their own right, and

OPPOSITE: **A large kitchen, where the cooking area is demarcated by a hefty island unit, reminiscent of a shop counter or apothecary's** chest. Old and new are on display, from the collection of copper pans that runs the length of the room to objects arranged on the island itself.

ABOVE: Colour is the link here: there is nothing on these dresser shelves that does not fit into the apple-green and white scheme.

RIGHT: Traditional earthenware in an equally traditional wire-fronted cupboard, where everything can be easily seen.

LEFT: A simple idea – a wire basket attached by butcher's hooks to a rail fixed above the work surface. Cutlery and utensils are to hand.

LEFT: **Although everything on display here is functional, it is all arranged so that it is seen at its stylish best.**

BELOW: **There is a traditional simplicity in old enamelled kitchenware and utensils, and a nostalgic charm.**

OPPOSITE ABOVE LEFT: **Jelly moulds – those most functional objects – take on a new life when displayed in a wall-hung glass case, where the ornamental detail of each mould can be appreciated.**

OPPOSITE ABOVE RIGHT: **Kitchen details don't have to be elaborate; a terracotta flowerpot is the perfect container for chunky cutlery.**

OPPOSITE BELOW LEFT: **A custom-made wooden box, hung on the wall to hold kitchen tools. Its plain lines accentuate the functional forms of the utensils.**

OPPOSITE BELOW RIGHT: **In a perfect combination of form and function, old celery glasses hold cutlery.**

storage jars – old enamel ones, new glass Kilner jars – always look inviting ranged together. Table linen adds softness to a room that can sometimes be hard-edged: coloured or patterned tablecloths and napkins, mats of different sizes and shapes, all add another dimension to flat surfaces – breakfast bars as well as tables.

Finally, look at the wall space. For a long time there seemed to be a convention that art was not appropriate for a kitchen, as a painting might be damaged by steam or grease; but while one might not hang an old master next to the cooker, inexpensive prints, photographs and posters will all add vivid life to the room.

plate racks and shelves

Some designs – the refectory table or a Windsor chair – are so perfect that they can never be bettered. Both the humble plate rack and the open shelf come into that category: functional, good-looking and a terrific use of space, they do the job now as well as they did 200 years ago. These days, plate racks are installed not merely to drain china that has been washed in the sink – although there can be few better ways of freeing up work surface space – but also as a way of displaying plates and dishes permanently. The open shelf is the most obliging of devices – able to fill an awkward corner or a tight space, to hold anything from bottles and jars to cups and saucers, with everything to hand. What would we do without them?

+ Mix open display shelving with closed, if you have some items in the kitchen – as most of us do – that are less attractive than others. Do not hesitate to put just the prettiest on show.

+ Too long a line of shelving can be boring and monotonous; break up the levels, or fit in short runs of shelving between other items of furniture.

+ There is no need to restrict plate racks to above the sink – a wide rack can take the place of a dresser, as it often did in old houses.

+ Open shelves are particularly effective if they are made of glass and hung in front of a window, so that they (and the items on them) seem to float.

+ Look for less obvious places where open shelving could be installed, such as above a door, high up around the kitchen walls, or along an adjoining corridor.

LEFT: A series of brightly coloured plates and an equally brightly coloured tray are stored so that they can be seen and enjoyed as well as used.

RIGHT: Cheap and cheerful; stacks of coloured glass tumblers, grouped together on open shelves among some cheerful kitsch items, become decorative objects in themselves.

A considered, sophisticated display at one end of the kitchen, with black lacquered open shelves holding an arrangement of opaque coloured glasses and large vases.

Colour adds enjoyment to our lives and enjoyment to a room – and vibrant colour even more so. Nowhere is this more true than in a hard-working kitchen.

colour in the kitchen

The kitchen is a busy place, so a neutral background, in the form of the finishes of units and worktop, is probably the best cooking environment, with splashes of colour injected in different forms, from fruit and vegetables to china and glass. There is something joyous about using colour in the kitchen; it speaks of pleasure and warmth – all good kitchen qualities. Even so, it is best used with a certain restraint – the odd laminated panel, perhaps, one bright painted wall or, if that is too much, added decorative details – pots and jugs, bottles and cushions, even cloths and napkins. If the kitchen is small, stick to touches of one strong tone and choose chrome and stainless steel for the main pieces of equipment; these are both good partners for colour, as they reflect other colours rather than adding to the mix.

A small kitchen lifted from the everyday with the injection of one strong colour – in this case, orange – in both the accessories and cooking ware.

living

If you are lucky enough to have, in any of your rooms, a fireplace and its attendant mantelpiece, you have in front of you one of the most perfect settings imaginable for all manner of decorative detail.

fireplaces and mantelpieces

In the 19th century, before the installation of central heating, and when almost every house had a fireplace, the decoration of the chimneypiece and its surrounds followed a widely accepted decorative convention. Tradition decreed that on the mantelshelf there might be – always in perfect symmetrical order – a selection of objects such as a central mirror, a pair of candelabra or candlesticks, a matching pair of flat-back figures or animals, and possibly a vase of flowers, all arranged the length of the shelf in a grouping that was both conventional and predictable.

Today, this set piece is no longer the norm; in fact, in many rooms, the fireplace and mantelpiece are almost completely ignored, often seemingly treated as part of

ABOVE LEFT: A carefully composed group of quirky and disparate objects that benefit from the simplicity of the white-painted, rather severe mantelpiece.

LEFT: The flamboyance of the orange and yellow tones in this strong picture is echoed and emphasized by the ceramic collection beneath.

OPPOSITE ABOVE LEFT AND RIGHT: A fireplace and mantelpiece designed out of strips of contrasting woods, deliberately left rough-hewn, form a fitting background for a collection of different wooden objects.

OPPOSITE BELOW: In this period panelled room in which the chimneypiece takes up a proportionately large amount of the fireplace wall, the mantelpiece display is deliberately kept restrained and subtle.

the wall, or even as a slight nuisance; things that occupy an otherwise useful space.

Actually, nothing could be further from the truth. A fireplace is, and has always been since the building of dwellings began, a natural central focus to a room; it represents physical warmth, of course, which in turn represents conviviality and hospitality. People naturally gravitate towards the fireplace, which is why a mantelpiece is such a perfect place to arrange and display collections and decorative objects of all types. It is the perfect setting for the quirky, the unusual, the treasured and the unique; a surface that is of perfect viewing height, with enough space above to create an interesting grouping, in a position that is a natural focus within the arrangement of the room.

If you are a collector, the idea of another display level is a really interesting one, as a mantelpiece or fireplace allows you the perfect opportunity to range and display a collection in a way that is low-key rather

ABOVE AND LEFT: In a country sitting room, this is a very personal and pretty arrangement for the mantelpiece. It is based around a collection of mirrors of different sizes, which have been combined with a variety of other objects chosen for their interesting shapes and design, such as the pieces of decorative plaster work and the antique iron scissors.

RIGHT: Against a background of silver-backed wallpaper, the mantelpiece is a home for a group of whimsical porcelain pieces.

This arrangement on the white-painted mantelpiece is more thoughtful than it may first appear; the deliberate inclusion of the spotted, dotted jug, making a direct link to the throw and cushion on the chair below, is both calculated and successful.

Nothing is allowed to disturb this excercise in white, and every part has been chosen for its colour and simplicity of design. The white-painted wooden mirror echoes the rest of the room and extends the eye upwards.

than 'look-at-me'. However, just as on a table or display shelf, height is an important factor – both the height of the objects on display and the proportional height of the wall and fireplace below. This idea can go further – the whole fireplace wall can be transformed with the addition of a mirror or picture that extends the eye upwards, and gives a new importance to the space. A mirror hung low can also extend space – it will reflect the objects in front of it, adding a further dimension.

For proportion is everything. Anything hung above must be in balance with the dimensions of the space below – both the fireplace itself as well as the mantelpiece – and should be strong enough to balance the black fireless hole that gapes below for several months of the year. If you fill the fireplace with something else in the warmer months, that too needs to be taken into consideration, as it will all be part of what the viewer sees as he or she enters the room.

The style of the mantelpiece and fire surround will affect what you display above it. Fragile ornaments will not look as good on a rustic shelf of old beams as similarly sturdy pieces, and vice versa: if your fireplace is an Adam surround, keep that balance in your mind as you choose the objects that you wish to display. This

LEFT: An old-fashioned stove in the fireplace sets the tone for a traditional group of small objects on the mantelpiece.

BELOW LEFT: A rough wood mantelshelf above a simple fireplace. Rightly, the shelf is used to display only a few equally simple objects.

BELOW: Almost sculptural in its design is this seemingly artless, but clever, grouping of objects, chosen primarily for shape and texture.

does not mean to say that on an 18th-century-inspired fireplace you can only display pieces of similar provenance or style; a contrast in style can be equally effective, as long as the overall mass is in proportion to the overall design. Interestingly, small pictures that are arranged to rest on the mantelshelf can be given a new importance, as shown in close-up, so to speak, they can be seen in a different light.

Lighting can also extend the decorative possibilities of a mantelpiece. Electric lighting might be in the form of wall lights – again positioned with care, and hung so that they light the shelf below as well as giving ambient light to the room. If the mantelpiece is sufficiently deep, stick-thin lamps on the mantelpiece itself can work, as of course can candles, massed together, or a pair in moderately imposing holders.

ABOVE: In a small room, a delightfully informal mantelpiece group with the classical oval convex mirror relating directly to the design of the mantelpiece. Note the witty, cut-out faux-flame solution in the empty grate.

LEFT: Not a tablescape, rather a mantelscape, with all the careful thought that that implies. Every element in the design is carefully planned as part of a greater whole, and the formal and striking group is extended beyond the mantelpiece itself to the wall on either side.

OPPOSITE: A country sitting room with a pleasing fireplace arrangement of personal things – photographs and invitations as well as decorative objects. The two groups of figures balance each other at either end of the mantelpiece.

For those with many
books, an over-door
shelf adds a pleasing
architectural dimension
to the room.

A remark often made about a cold or impersonal room is that it doesn't look 'lived-in', because no books are to be seen; books are indeed a necessary part of our lives.

living with books

In many ways books, both old and new, do more to personalize and humanize a room than almost any other detail or accessory. The key word here is probably 'personal'; however pleasing the variety of colour, size, typeface and design, what gives books their most lasting and most widespread appeal is the sense that they are there because those who live with them enjoy using them and reading them. Books that have been bought for their overall dimensions, or to be admired rather than read, seem to possess an intangible air of neglect and almost sadness.

One should not perhaps be too precious in arranging books in a room. They look good when seen in profusion, not arranged with military precision in

TOP LEFT: A modest double bookshelf set high on the wall is in perfect proportion and scale to the sofa beneath.

ABOVE LEFT: Since part of the joy of books is their varied and often beautiful appearance, a carefully arranged stack can be very satisfying to the eye.

ABOVE: A free-form wall-hanging bookshelf, securing the books between metal restraints.

LEFT: A storage solution that is practical, portable and smart; what could almost be described as a book bench, with the upper surface free for coffee and drinks and the inner shelf filled with books.

RIGHT: Clever planning and design have resulted in an ingenious and good-looking architectural solution to the book storage problem; a mini-library, where a wide space connecting two rooms has been adjusted to make two inner sets of bookshelves that are linked to the pair of conventional bookcases either side.

neatly colour-coded piles like sweaters, or graded to precise dimensions. They are at their best when accessible at a glance, arranged to some loose, usually personal, classification system, and stored not only on shelves, but on tables and even the floor. Accessible does not, in this instance, mean 'immediately to hand'; in book land, as long as you can actually see the book, you are secure in the knowledge that it is there.

Wherever books are stored, they should be, in their own context, tidily arranged and well-kept; it is disturbing to see them kept any which way, never mind upside-down and open beneath another volume. Such treatment implies a lack of respect or care for their contents as well as their outer appearance, and that is something no book lover can bear to see.

Many of those who love and buy books quickly come to despair of how to arrange and display their usually ever-expanding collection. Here lateral thinking can be useful: books do not have to be kept all together in large bookcases or custom-made shelves; they can be stored everywhere there is a convenient wall space – above a

OPPOSITE: In a small room, with little space for storage, a double set of bookshelves: one conventional and holding larger volumes; the other designed to face the bed, with smaller volumes ready to hand.

ABOVE RIGHT: When it is closed, the mirrored door that faces these tall

bookshelves reflects the colour and variety of the volumes towards the rest of the room.

BELOW RIGHT: In a contemporary loft space is this set of sturdy, metal, wall-hung bookshelves, each on a central stem. They can be erected wherever there is a little extra space to spare.

door or a pair of doors, perhaps, or in a narrow corridor linking two rooms. A door that has been sealed could become a tall, shallow set of shelves for paperbacks, and a dead space above a cupboard can house a purpose-built shelf for books of a particular size.

Piles of books can act as lamp tables beside sofas and chairs, and books can transform a traditional dining room, particularly if it is dominated by a largish table. Arranged in stacks of different heights and dimensions, perhaps combined with a table light and a bowl of flowers, the table, and by definition the room itself, becomes a welcoming place to be used at any time of day. This concept can be extended past the table: a room that is only occasionally used for dining can work well transformed into a book room, with bookcases on several walls; nothing is nicer than eating in the evening, preferably by candlelight, surrounded by books.

The idea of books being part of a display, rather than merely items to store neatly, leads to the loosely related idea of bookshelves and bookcases as display cabinets. Firstly, the volumes themselves can be arranged in the shelves in blocks of different widths and heights, some set upright, others face up, to make a loose geometric design. If the shelves are divided into sections, think of leaving some sections free of books and using the space to hold other things, from a plant to a pretty object, or a piece of china or glass; if the bookcase is

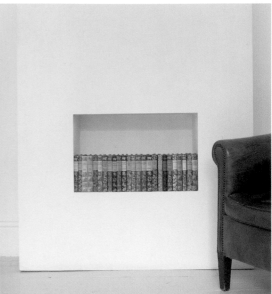

of painted wood, think of painting the inner sides of the shelves a darker colour than the outer shell, to emphasize the frame idea. If the shelves are not divided, you can still break up the lines of books with decorative punctuation between groups. Use the confines of the shelf, and the sides of the books, as frames for a quirky object, an old box, or even a small figurative or sculptural piece.

Another pleasing display idea is to incorporate pictures into shelves of books; again using empty sections of shelf to house a picture, hung or propped against the wall, or hanging pictures on the uprights. Although this does somewhat limit the number and size of the volumes you can store behind the picture, it is, visually, most effective and brings the bookshelves into the overall decorative scheme of the room.

ABOVE LEFT: **A satisfying sight: a bookcase made to measure in traditional style, with shelves above and cupboards below, painted friendly olive green and housing intriguing volumes on every shelf.**

TOP RIGHT: **Stored in what was once a fireplace, a matching set of volumes in different-coloured jackets becomes a decorative detail in its own right.**

ABOVE RIGHT: **Even an awkwardly shaped room has space, somewhere, for a bookshelf. In this attic room, books are ranged beneath the sloping roof.**

OPPOSITE: **Everything in this room is carefully chosen and in period – 20th-century classicism. The pleasingly solid functional bookshelves, and the manner in which the volumes are arranged, are in keeping with the whole.**

OPPOSITE ABOVE LEFT:
Is it function, or is it art? This cheery and clever shade for a kitchen ceiling light makes what is often considered as a design black hole into a witty statement.

OPPOSITE ABOVE RIGHT:
A traditional design, these weighted pulley ceiling lights are a perfect solution to the perennial problem of how to light a dining table so that the light illuminates the food rather than the diners.

OPPOSITE BELOW LEFT:
A decorative blown-glass light becomes part of a group, partnered with white decorative ceramic vases.

OPPOSITE BELOW RIGHT:
Both functional and decorative is this pair of angled reading lamps, hung from the wall in a work room.

The lighting and light fittings that you choose for every room have as much to do with decorative detail as they have to do with function and practicality.

lighting

Lighting today is a vast subject, immensely technical, and with new developments continually being produced. Lighting designers – those who understand these intricate technicalities as well as the general art of good lighting – say that all lighting should be treated as a whole, in the same way as you would think about the colours and furnishings of a room. This is of course the right approach, but it should not deter you from looking at individual lights as important details in a room, details that have a dual purpose – that not only stand on their own merit as interesting and appealing objects, but which also add to the way that that room is lit at different times.

These lights may be just beautiful or decorative, and they may be functional also – task lighting, as it is known; they may even feature as ambient lighting, lighting that fills the background of a room with warmth and defines the space. The important thing is that you

A group of tea lights in assorted glass tumblers makes an easy and charming pool of light on a table.

An adjustable floor reading light is an essential in a room with comfortable chairs. This slender version is smart but also self-effacing.

ABOVE: **A clear glass cylinder lamp base is perfectly matched with the strong ceramic shapes grouped around it on the table.**

ABOVE RIGHT: **On a white-painted table, there is a textural contrast between the fragile glass drops of the candelabrum and the adjacent simple, white-glazed jugs.**

RIGHT: **Like flying saucers, three ceiling lights, all slightly different in shape and all hung at different heights, illuminate a stairwell.**

find the right place for each light in the broader design scheme, somewhere that both shows them to advantage and adds to the overall charm of the setting. Give thought to the dimensions of each light. Table lights should be in scale with the surface area they stand on, chandeliers should always be hung lower rather than higher, and floor lamps should not impede the furniture or your progress around the room.

Lighting might take the form of table lamps, wall lamps, floor lamps, chandeliers or candlesticks. They may be old or they may be new, converted from something else or individually designed; they may stand on their own in solitary splendour, or work better as part of a wider group. Whatever their style, try them out first in different places in the room to see where they will have most impact – and don't forget to have dimmer switches installed wherever possible.

The effervescent beauty of the chandelier is once again admired and enjoyed; this charming example mixes clear with coloured pendant drops and is hung so that it is reflected in the overmantel mirror.

adaptable lampshades

Along with cushions, professional interior decorators always like to focus on lampshades as the way to a quick decorative pick-me-up. To them, lampshades are a bit like skirt lengths: often, barely perceptible changes make all the difference to the look. Where you might add or subtract an inch on a hem, so on a lamp you might replace a drum shade with a coolie shape, a circular frame with a rectangular one. To continue the fashion analogy, it is these small differences of silhouette that alter the style of the whole lamp and how it is perceived in decoration terms. Colour, too, is an important weapon in the decorative arsenal. Acres of cream lampshades, whether in pleated silk, plain card or vellum, may be safe, but they are also very dull; to avoid a sea of serene blandness, use colour, and use pattern – think of each lamp and its shade as a decorative entity rather than just a practical necessity.

✦ Contrast of texture is important between a lamp and its shade. If the base is metal, for example, find a shade that is made from something different and that has a softer quality.

✦ Lining the shade with a coloured silk will alter the quality of the light, making it softer or deeper.

✦ It is amusing to embellish lampshades with bits of decorative ornament, which can be as temporary as you like. Ribbon or braid can be stuck around the base, glass droplets can be hung from the shade, clip-on butterflies and birds have a certain, if finite, charm, and so do strings of beads, garlanded around.

✦ If you have more than a couple of table lamps in a room, ensure that they are of varied heights, so that you avoid a flat wash of light at one level.

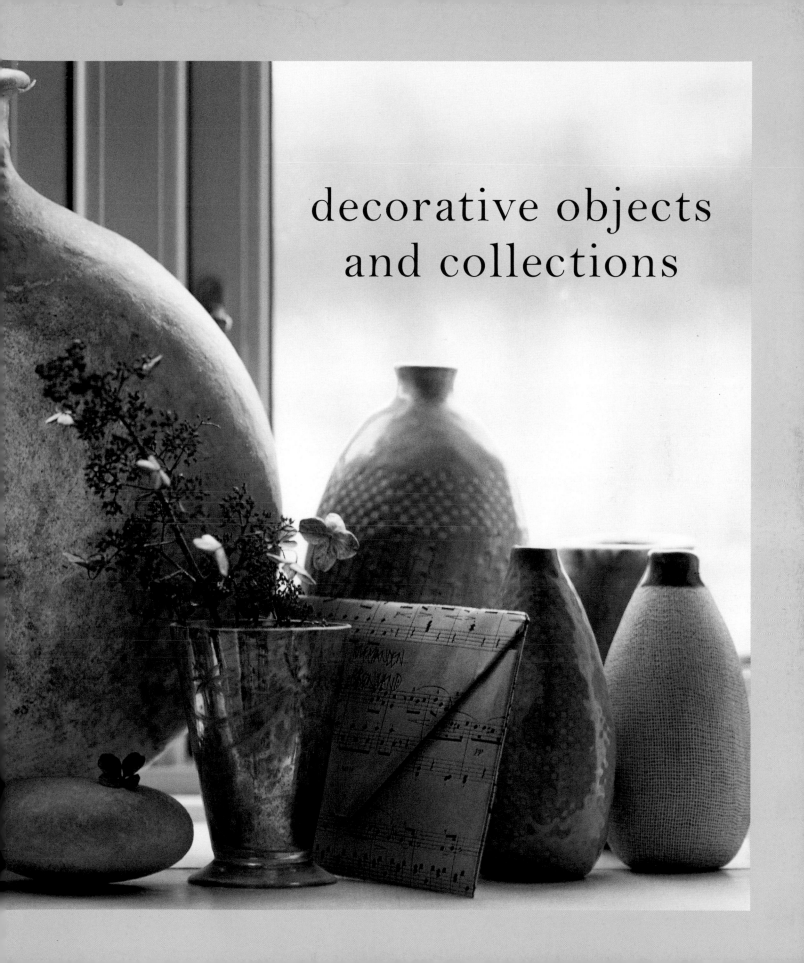

decorative objects
and collections

We are all natural collectors, whether we know it or not, and every collection, in all its detail, large or small, deserves to be shown off to its very best advantage.

creative collections

Although it might be stretching a point to say that everybody collects something, most of us, over time, amass – even unconsciously – collections of one thing or another, whether they are based on the absolutely practical or the purely ornamental. And all collections, whether premeditated or not, come under the heading of interior details; each one is a unique visual statement that adds enormously to the overall impact of a room.

The first step, of course, is to identify what exactly your particular collection, or collections, might consist of. It may simply be several examples of a type of thing that pleases you, like the printed fabric bags and necklaces shown here; or it might be a field of fine art in which you have researched and searched out pieces

ABOVE: The simplest of groupings: a clutch of bags, each made from a different antique chintz, hung from an old coat rack above the bed.

LEFT: On a bench just above floor level is a group of small wooden pieces, each as chunky as the bench below.

RIGHT: An example of how one collection can enhance another: delicate glass beads below the shelf; equally delicate coloured-base glass vases above.

When a collection has an intrinsic artistic value, it should be displayed in a manner that reflects its worth. Here a group of fine sculptural pieces is displayed in an open cabinet, with each object set in its own frame.

over many years. Not all collections are about a particular genre of object or even a

single maker; collections can be based on a period – Art Deco or Georgian; a material

– bone, ivory, wood, ceramic; a technique – turned wood, etched glass or bead work.

Whatever the theme and whichever end of the scale, it is important to work out how

to show your collection or collections at their most homogeneous best.

The art of collecting is closely linked to the art of display. Most people like their

collections to be seen and admired, and a collection hidden behind doors and kept in

boxes is a sad and unloved thing. So take it out and look it over, and think about how

ABOVE: **Everyday objects have a beauty and a charm that comforts as they please. A collection of traditional earthenware pots and jugs is wittily displayed in a series of open wooden packing boxes.**

OPPOSITE LEFT: **Antique ivory dressing tools – including brushes and glove stretcher – are laid out around an antique dressing-table mirror.**

OPPOSITE RIGHT: **Old wooden glove and boot moulds are kept in a woven basket; the contrast of texture is very pleasing.**

A charming collection of old hand mirrors of every size, age and material is simply displayed on a wall, each one hung in a slightly different manner, some with handle up, some down, some with glass hidden, others with glass revealed; the whole makes an unusual and interesting composition.

to display the group in a manner which is both attractive and which adds to the overall impact of the room.

Styles and fashions in display have changed over the centuries. Paintings were once hung almost at ceiling height, often cantilevered forwards, and decorative ceramic objects or pieces of sculpture were crammed very closely together, to be admired as much for their rich profusion as for their beauty. Today, however, we live in (decoratively) simpler times, and what pleases us visually is an unspoken sense of space, with furniture and belongings arranged to emphasize that – which means, in terms of a collection, that the space between the objects is as important as their visual balance.

ABOVE: **Textile hand-printing blocks – every one different, and all of them old – make an intensely satisfying composition when arranged almost like a picture. One block on its own would not have the same impact.**

RIGHT: **A white-painted cupboard used as a frame for two separate compositions, one pale and one dark. Ranged side by side, they balance each other out.**

OPPOSITE: **The visual weight of the silvered bottles and jars above the cupboard is balanced by the piles of textiles and, on the upper shelf, flasks, stored inside the cupboard.**

The manner in which a collection is displayed adds hugely to its appeal, which is why space, proportion, balance and light are necessary. Each piece should be shown in harmony with what is around it, whether they are pieces of furniture, furnishings or decorative objects, and each piece must make a pleasing visual composition in conjunction with its neighbours.

A group of objects has a stronger impact, not only on each other, but also on the room in which they are displayed; they become a mass, equal in stature to other pieces in the room. Although we no longer want to display a collection very densely, it is within a group that one sees the point of any collection – the differences and variations between the designs. Grouping them reinforces the relationship between each piece in a way that serried ranks of objects would not.

ABOVE LEFT: **A confident composition of natural and naturally influenced objects, this arrangement could be the basis for a still-life painting.**

BELOW: **A collection of red and white household textiles** becomes something attractive to look at as well as to use.

OPPOSITE: **Not just a linen cupboard: these household linens have been arranged as much for aesthetics as for their practicality.**

A collection of white-glazed pots, all with relief decoration, makes an impact because of the number and the variety of designs.

This vast collection of antique, porcelain tureens has been arranged in the simplest of styles, so that each different design can be appreciated in individual isolation.

Some collections group together easily, particularly smaller pieces and those items that are not striking individually, but which gain importance when grouped with others of that ilk. Larger objects must be given enough air to breathe properly; crammed together, they get lost and have no individuality. And the more ornate and complex they are, the more air they need. Large pieces must be balanced by pieces of equal weight, and very strong pieces should perhaps be shown in isolation, with other parts of the collection given equal prominence elsewhere. It's all to do with the correct use of scale.

The immediate setting for the collection, whether it is the surface on which the pieces stand or a background, is important. Light pieces on a dark ground work well, and vice versa; a textured background often works well, too, and a contrast of textures can be striking, as long as it does not deflect attention from what is on display.

BELOW: **Not just a collection, but a composition, combining sculpted heads with circular and oval plates, all in the same palette.**

RIGHT: Celadon green pottery, combined with a small seascape that echoes the grey-green tones of the vases.

BELOW: Antique glazed earthenware dishes, simply hung on the wall in a way that allows both the differences and similarities of the designs to be seen.

In many cases, one collection can be displayed with another, an effective device but one which is only successful when they share either a narrative or a visual context. They must also be of comparative weight – to combine a collection of African masks with glass scent bottles would be counter-productive. If displaying more than one collection at the same time, think about contrasting textures – hard with soft, cool with hot. All successful display, and for that matter decoration, is a matter of juxtaposition; this is not as hard as it might sound, for the beauty of most collections – unless they are steam engines or dinosaur skeletons – is that the pieces can be tried first in one place and then in another until the result gives pleasure to collector and viewer alike.

ABOVE: **Old tea tins, with their imaginative designs, full of colour and life, are ranged close together on the kitchen shelf.**

OPPOSITE: **Even the most functional objects, like these old hat moulds, can look striking when grouped together. On a green-painted wall between two windows, they make a strong, witty statement.**

LEFT: **A group linked together both by colour and by period, mostly mid-20th century. Much careful thought has been put into the actual arrangement, both shelf by shelf and as an overall composition.**

ABOVE: **Coloured glass always looks good grouped together, and it always looks best in front of a window, where the shapes stand out against the light.**

Creating an arrangement of small objects of desire on a table or desktop, where all can admire them, is a deeply satisfying thing to do and as easy, after all, as banishing them to a dark cupboard or drawer.

tablescapes

It was the late David Hicks, one of the most influential decorators of the 20th century, who coined the term 'tablescapes' to describe the display and arrangement of objects – often disparate – grouped together on a side table or some other low, relatively small surface. In the same way that he used unusual, often bright contrasts of colour and texture in his rooms – at the time, a totally new kind of decorative style – so his tablescapes were intended to make those who saw them look at the chosen objects with new interest. It was the juxtaposition of the unusual and the unobvious that Hicks was interested in, and that holds just as good today as it did then; his skilful groupings relied also on the balancing of objects of different weights and volume, and he rearranged these scenes often, sometimes every day; a step too far for most of us, perhaps, but his aim was always to find something new, alive and interesting in a room, and to convey that sense to other people.

Most of us have odd objects languishing in cupboards – the stray bit of china, the remaining candlestick of what was once a pair, a pretty box too

ABOVE: **An old painted games table with a group that picks up the tones of the design of the table; two old books make a plinth for the recumbent figure.**

LEFT: **A corner of a feminine room is made even more so by a group that includes 18th-century portraits, ribbons and scent.**

RIGHT: **A very assured and interesting table- or rather deskscape, which incorporates the top of the desk as well as the lower writing surface. A collection of animal figures is combined with old photographs in decorative frames, as well as a lamp and flowers and an embossed Victorian picture album.**

small to keep anything in; they are there not because we don't like them, but because we just don't know what to do with them or how to show them off in an attractive way. The first step towards creating a tablescape is to get out these bits and pieces and look at them dispassionately, rather as one might look at pictures waiting to be hung, and then move them into loose groups to see what combinations, if any, catch your eye and might work together. You might for example find that you have two old coffee cups with gilded borders, or one small white bowl and a non-matching white jug; put them together, and see what else in your group of objets trouvés might work in tandem. Then look around and think what else you have that is already on display – a clock, a book, a small picture, a vase – and think about whether they could be brought into the group to good effect.

Initially, a thematic approach of colour, subject or material might be a good one. The idea is to make a group that has a certain visual weight; and height, proportion and balance are the keys to successful arrangements. Although you will strive for interesting juxtapositions, there should also be a certain harmony and relationship between the things you put together.

OPPOSITE: **A strong, almost painterly, and very precise composition, arranged on a polished table. A print with another image layered over it, an oversized laboratory flask holding the stems of a climbing flower, and all the other, unrelated objects are arranged with symmetry and regularity.**

ABOVE RIGHT: **A comfortable, friendly tablescape with Eastern overtones, exemplified by the elephant and camel figures as well as the model of the Taj Mahal. Books are used to give height to the pieces.**

RIGHT: **An arrangement based purely on balance and scale. There is no linking theme between any of these objects, except their harmonious proportions.**

Tablescapes often benefit from the inclusion of plants or flowers, as well as other natural objects such as ornamental gourds and seed heads, shells and even fossils.

The surface on which you arrange your chosen objects is obviously of prime importance. Tablecloths, particularly floor-length examples, now seem rather fussy and old-fashioned; better to use as a background the natural surface of the table or desktop, whether it is wood, stone or some other surface. Lighting is another important element of a tablescape. You could incorporate directional lighting that focuses down onto the group; alternatively, a table lamp of the right size, or candlesticks or candelabra, will all give definition to the scene.

A well-grouped tablescape also has another role, playing as it does a part in the interior design of the room, as well as its decoration: a table in a corner, for example, draws the eye outwards to the edges of the room, while a table between two chairs or behind a sofa takes the eye beyond the table display to the pieces of furniture around it.

LEFT: A rustic and informal group: on an old painted and distressed table, the pieces are in keeping with the background – earthenware, candles, dried fruit and flowers and a black-framed mirror propped up behind.

ABOVE: Another pleasingly informal group. A polished round table is the setting for an old mirror, a reel of twine, a wine bottle holding a single allium stem, and various shells in an old jar.

A window is always a good backdrop for a table arrangement. These objects on a low table have been chosen purely for their pleasing dimensions; an old nautical instrument, some natural objects, an old album and a mismatched pair of plants in pots.

In a witty take on display storage, and a clever idea where space is limited, metal dressmaking dummies or shop window mannequins have been hung as a group on the bedroom wall and then decorated with a collection of beads and artificial flowers.

Conceived purely and simply as personal decoration, jewellery is the one craft – or art – that should never be allowed to hide its sparkling light under a bushel. Show it off wherever and whenever possible.

jewellery

What's wonderful about jewellery, and why everyone loves it, is that, on the whole, it has no practical purpose at all – unless you could define its purpose as being to adorn and beautify as well as bringing pleasure to both the wearer and the spectator. Adornment in the form of jewellery has been made for almost as long as man has been on earth. Shell jewellery has been found dating from the Middle Stone Age, and both the Egyptians and the Greeks used gold, glass, stones and enamel in creating what are still stunningly beautiful bracelets, rings, collars, necklaces and earrings. Most of us seem to have the magpie and jackdaw gene – we are attracted to bright, sparkly things – and we love to collect them, sometimes in an almost haphazard manner.

Although primarily thought of as a personal, fashionable detail, jewellery has a part to play in adding decorative detail around the house. We are probably not speaking here of major pieces, the sort of things that require secure surroundings and padded boxes; rather, we are speaking about those

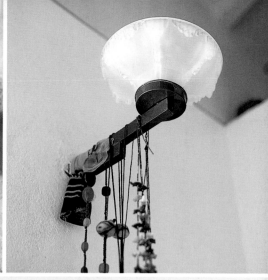

An oriental ornamental tree, usually made from semi-precious stones like rose quartz, has been further embellished with pairs of earrings hung from its branches.

ABOVE LEFT: **A cushion covered in antique toile has been skewered with a collection of brooches,** carefully chosen to complement the fabric's two-tone design.

ABOVE RIGHT: **With great ingenuity, this lamp wired into the wall has been commandeered, to good effect, into acting as a storage rail for a group of bead necklaces.**

LEFT: Old-fashioned small ring trees, and larger jewellery trees made in the form of hands with elongated fingers, were very popular in the 19th century. This pair displays bangles and bracelets.

BELOW: The edge of a mirror is always a good place to store beads and necklaces; here, their charm is increased by the addition of some flowers to the picture.

OPPOSITE: A jewellery-inspired tablescape, and a very feminine one; a hand-painted and gilded coffee pot and cup have been further embellished by costume jewellery – a necklace draped over the cup, a ring on the spout of the pot.

ABOVE: A contemporary take on the ring tree: metal cones that are precisely the right width for a collection of silver rings.

pieces, often flimflam, that bring a little glamour, pleasure and twinkle into life. Jewellery works well used as a little extra adornment to other more mundane household objects – a string of pearls or ribbon of beads hung over a lampshade, wound round the neck of a plain vase, garlanded along a mantelpiece or hung at the bottom of a blind; and bigger, more solid pieces used in larger table groupings – a pile of silver bangles next to a vase of white roses or framed miniature.

And then there is the idea of display storage: instead of keeping your pieces in drawers and boxes (where you often forget what is where), hang beads from hooks and knobs, rings on ring trees or hands (which can be found antique and new and in both glass and porcelain), and stick earrings and brooches in pin cushions and miniature pillows. The benefit is that, since jewellery looks even nicer in profusion than in isolation, you can both admire and wear your favourite pieces.

RIGHT: What could be simpler? Sometimes less is more: a line of sea-smoothed pebbles set out along a windowsill, each one ready both to look at and pick up.

BELOW: A striking and unusual piece of coral, so much so that it has been mounted on a stand and displayed as part of a simple but effective grouping.

OPPOSITE ABOVE RIGHT: A raft made from a piece of rock makes a soothing combination, with two polished pebbles and a weathered piece of driftwood.

OPPOSITE FAR RIGHT: Two fine ammonites are balanced by a group of fossilized leaves mounted on a board, and carefully chosen pebbles.

OPPOSITE RIGHT: The simpler, the better – a grey-glazed dish with a collection of different-coloured pebbles and flat scallop shells.

OPPOSITE BELOW LEFT: In a bathroom, between the salts and scents, a fragile sea urchin's shell and two shell balls, and jars of shells.

OPPOSITE BELOW RIGHT: Everyday Atlantic sea shells heaped in a bowl are just as pretty to look at as their more exotic Southern counterparts.

The beauty and wonder of natural objects, from fossils to shells, coral to pebbles, is timeless and ageless. It is no wonder that we still like to see them around us, wherever we live.

shells and other natural objects

The Age of Enlightenment, that period dating from the 18th century when the interest in natural sciences was at its height, was a time when exploratory expeditions were raised and men travelled the known world, returning to Europe with sketches and specimens of exotic plants, minerals, shells and fossils. Collectors filled cabinets of curiosity with examples of such things, fired by a fascination to learn more about the natural world. That fascination continues today – we are still enchanted by the beauty of a shell, a polished pebble or the outline of a fossilized leaf, preserved for thousands of years, and we like to own and display such pieces in our homes. The right place to show off such treasures is near to eye level, so that their unique beauty can be appreciated at close quarters.

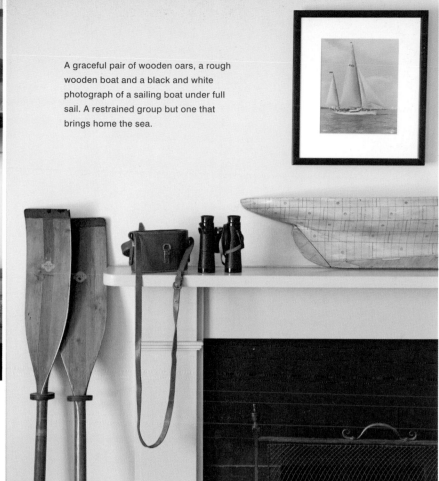

A graceful pair of wooden oars, a rough wooden boat and a black and white photograph of a sailing boat under full sail. A restrained group but one that brings home the sea.

OPPOSITE: A beautiful wooden sailing ship with full rigging; intricate enough to be seen in all its majesty in front of an undressed window.

ABOVE: As all anglers know, flies and floats are a subject of endless fascination, almost a folk art, and this row of fishing-line floats look at their best hung from a simple wooden block.

'I must down to the seas again, to the lonely sea and the sky,
And all I ask is a tall ship and a star to steer her by,
And the wheel's kick and the wind's song and the white sail's shaking,
And a grey mist on the sea's face and a grey dawn breaking.'

BELOW: In a corner of a child's bedroom are the beginnings of a nautical collection, with a fisherman's boat on the wall and a simple block of wood, carved and painted into shipshape form.

ships and boats

In his famous poem *Sea Fever*, John Masefield encapsulated the romantic feeling that many people have about all things nautical. From childhood we like to collect objects that pertain to the sea, from bathtime boats to mystifying ships in bottles. Painstakingly made boats, large and small, abound not only in antique shops, but also as new versions; many of them are instant heirlooms, beautiful enough to be displayed far from the confines of the bathroom. The only way *not* to display anything remotely nautical is to go down the theme park road. Everything to do with working with or living on water has a refined and functional beauty about it, and such artefacts are best viewed in relative isolation, rather than being linked by lobster pots or, heaven forbid, draped and swagged fishing nets.

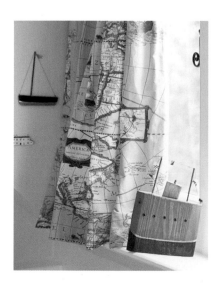

Whether it is a pleasant nostalgia for a happy childhood or simply an interest in the craftsmanship and imagination of early toymakers, most people are intrigued by old toys, and like to see them on display.

LEFT: There is a simplicity of form in early toys that gives them an enormous charm, particularly as here when several are ranged together.

BELOW LEFT: An old rocking horse, particularly one that shows the patina of age and use, is a wonderful thing to own, at any age.

vintage toys

For both adults and children alike, it is hard to resist the lure of an old toy, particularly when it is happened upon unexpectedly, placed somewhere you might not think to see it. A painted wooden rocking horse standing in a bay window, a chair with an old doll sitting in it, a shelf with an arrangement of small lead figures waiting endlessly on a platform for a train that will never come; all catch the eye and add interest to a room. Many heirloom toys, particularly those that were handmade, are works of art, and have a sculptural quality about them that makes them as eligible for serious display as any more grown-up figure or form. Display your vintage toys with circumspection and avoid, without fail, any hint of the whimsical or cute; they deserve better than that.

BELOW: Many 20th-century toys have as much charm as older models. This group, which includes a Mexican papier-mâché doll as well as different sets of contemporary stacking dolls, is bright and colourful.

A collection of early toys that is still in use. Each has a distinct personality, from the rugged wooden castle on the floor to the much-loved threadbare dog on wheels, and good, old-fashioned noisy drum. It would be a shame to hide any of these behind cupboard doors.

index

Figures in *italics* indicate photographs.

business credits

Architects, designers and businesses whose work has been featured in this book.

A

An Angel At My Table
Painted and French furniture specialists.
+44 0845 2000723
www.anangelatmytable.com
Page 94al

Annabel Grey
+44 07860 500356
annabel.grey@btinternet.com
www.annabelgrey.com
Pages 85, 124br, 132, 136–137

Annelie Bruijn
+31 653 702869
Annelie_bruijn@email.com
Pages 73br, 100a, 134ar

Anthropologie
+1 800 309 2500
www.anthropologie.com
Page 18a

Asfour Guzy Architects
594 Broadway, Suite 1204
New York, NY 10012
+1 212 334 9350
info@asfourguzy.com
www.asfourguzy.com
Page 27bl

Asplund (Showroom and Shop)
Sibyllegatan 31
114 42 Stockholm, Sweden
+46 8 662 52 84
www.asplund.org
Page 75al

Atelier Abigail Ahern
137 Upper Street
London N1 1QP
+44 020 7354 8181
contact@atelierbypost.com
www.atelierabigailahern.com
Pages 32, 50–51, 58l

B

Baileys
Whitecross Farm, Bridstow
Herefordshire HR9 6JU
+44 01989 561931
www.baileys-home-garden.co.uk
*Pages 2cr, 7al, 9, 101a both,
105br, 126, 129bl, 129br, 134br,
147al*

Baroque Garden
www.baroquegarden.com
Page 113a

Beach Studios
+44 01797 344077
www.beachstudios.co.uk
*Pages 1, 2cl, 24b, 27a, 31br,
38br, 47ar, 65, 66b, 67ar, 67br,
79l, 93al, 94br, 102a, 102bl,
149ar, 160*

Ben de Lisi
40 Elizabeth Street
London SW1 9NZ
+44 020 7730 2994
Page 125

Ben Pentreath
Working Group Design and
Ben Pentreath Ltd (Shop)
17 Rugby Street
London WC1N 3QT
www.working-group.co.uk
Pages 33bl, 33ar

Bennison Fabrics Ltd
16 Holbein Place
London SW1W 8NL
+44 020 7730 6781
www.bennisonfabrics.com
Page 36al, 61b,124a

Bexon Woodhouse Creative
+44 01531 630176
www.bexonwoodhouse.com
Pages 75ar,101b,138a

Bois-Renard
Decorative home accessories.
+1 215 247 4777
Page 127a

Brissi Contemporary Living
196 Westbourne Grove
London W11 2RH
+44 020 7727 2159
info@brissi.co.uk
www.brissi.co.uk
Pages 104, 116bl, 118ar

C

Caroline Zoob
www.caroline-zoob.co.uk
Page 151br

Catherine Malandrino
www.catherinemalandrino.com
Page 96bl

Cecilia Proserpio
cecilia.proserpio@fastwebnet.it
Page 93bl

Chambre d'Amis
www.chambredamis.com
Page 76r

Charlotte Casadejus
www.charlottecasadejus.com
Page 64bl

Charmaine and Paul Jack
Interior Architecture
and Design
LESUD Design
lesudchar@wanadoo.fr
Pages 23bl, 142l

**The Children's Cottage
Company**
Devon
+44 01363 772061
www.play-houses.com
and Sanctuary Garden Offices
Devon
+44 01363 772061
www.sanctuarygardenoffices.com
Pages 84al, 138–139

**Christophe Ducharme,
Architecte**
15 rue Hégésippe Moreau
75018 Paris, France
+33 01 45 22 07 75
Pages 13, 45l

**Claes Bech-Poulsen,
Photographer**
+45 40 19 93 99
claes@claesbp.com
www.claesbp.dk
Pages 117a, 129a

Colin Orchard Consultants
London, +44 020 7720 7550
info@colinorchard.com
Pages 11, 141b

Cote Jardin
Boutique: Place du Marché
17590 Ars en Ré, France
Pages 142r, 151al

Crème de la Crème à la Edgar
Kompagnistræde 8, St
1208 Copenhagen K, Denmark
+45 33361818
Pages 41l, 80ar

The Cross
141 Portland Road
London W11 4LR
and Cross the Road
139 Portland Road
+44 020 7727 6760
Page 120br

D

Davy Hezemans, Spice PR
Leidsegracht 38–40
1016 CM – Amsterdam
+31 65 530 0375
Page 109r

Design By Us
www.design-by-us.com
www.villalagachon.com
Summer house to rent in France.
Page 150

The Dodo
www.thedodo.co.uk
Pages 67al, 149br

Domaine de la Baronnie
21 Rue Baron de Chantal
17410 Saint-Martin-de-Ré
France
+33 5 46 09 21 29
www.labaronnie-pallardy.com
Page 67bl

E

Eero Aarnio
www.eero-aarnio.com
Fax: +35 89 25 68 547
Page 118al

Elizabeth Baer Textiles
+44 01225 866136
dbaer@onetel.com
Pages 127bl, 131

Emily Chalmers, Author/Stylist
emily@emilychalmers.com
Shop: Caravan
3 Redchurch Street
Shoreditch, London E1 7DJ
+44 020 7247 6467
www.caravanstyle.com
Pages 36br, 40l

Emma Bridgewater
739 Fulham Road
London SW6 5UL
+44 020 7371 5489
www.emmabridgewater.co.uk
Page 19ar

Emma Greenhill
egreenhill@freenet.co.uk
Pages 38ar, 44r

F

Fil de Fer
St. Kongensgade 83 A
1264 Copenhagen K, Denmark
+45 33 32 32 46
www.fildefer.dk
Page 31bl

Francesca Mills
www.francescamills.com
Pages 46,108

Françoise de Nobele Antiquitès
2 rue de Bourbon le Chateau
75006 Paris, France
Page 133bl

French Country Living
Antiques and decoration.
21 rue de l'Eglise
06250 Mougins, France
+ 33 4 93 75 53 03
f.c.l.com@wanadoo.fr
Page 91br

G

Gabriella Abbado, Designer
+39 333 90 30 809
Pages 23br, 145ar

Grethe Meyer
Designer and architect MAA
Royal Scandinavia A/S
+45 38144848
www.royalscandinavia.com
Pages 2ar, 88–89, 95r

Gul Coskun, Coskun Fine Art
91–93 Walton Street
London SW3 2HP
+44 020 7581 9056
www.coskunfineart.com
Pages 2bl, 70al

Guy Hills, Photographer
www.guyhills.com
Page 91bl

H

Haifa Hammami, Architect
+44 07730 307612
Page 115

Het Grote Avontuur
Haarlemmerstraat 25
1013 EJ Amsterdam
The Netherlands
+31 206268597
www.hetgroteavontuur.nl
Page 47br

Hilary Robertson
No. Eight, 8 East Parade
Hastings, Sussex TN34 3AL
+44 01424 443521
www.noeight.co.uk
Alistair McGowan
West Matravers
+44 07770 765106
al@westmatravers.com
Pages 2ac, 29r, 144

Historic Buildings Consultants
8 Doughty Mews
London WC1N 2PG
+44 020 7831 4398
www.hbcconsultants.com
Page 106b

Hotel Endsleigh
Milton Abbot, Tavistock, Devon
+44 01822 870000
www.hotelendsleigh.com
Page 2c

Hôtel Le Sénéchal
6 rue Gambetta
17590 Ars en Ré, France
+33 05 46 29 40 42
www.hotel-le-senechal.com
Pages 13, 45l

Hotel Tresanton, Cornwall
+44 01326 270055
www.tresanton.com
Page 151ar

Household Hardware
www.householdhardware.nl
Pages 56a, 96ar

Hunt Slonem
545 West 45th Street, 4th Floor
New York, NY 10036
+1 212 620 4835
www.huntslonem.com
Pages 23a, 77b

I

Ilaria Miani
Shop: Via Monserrato, 35
00186 Roma, Italy
+39 0668 33160
ilariamiani@tin.it
Podere Casellacce and Podere
Buon Riposo in Val d'Orcia are
available to rent.
Pages 110–111

J

Jamb Limited
Antique chimneypieces.
Core One, The Gas Works
Gate D, Michael Road
London SW6 2AN
+44 020 7736 3006
www.jamblimited.com
Page 116br

Jan Constantine
+44 01270 821194
www.janconstantine.com
Pages 71r, 143

Jane Packer
www.janepacker.com
*Pages 7ar, 14–15, 36ar, 42, 83al,
91ar, 148a*

Jette Arendal Winther
www.arendal-ceramics.com
Pages 7b, 10

Joanne Cleasby
At Snoopers Paradise
7–8 Kensington Gardens
Brighton BN1 4AL
+44 01273 602558
Page 134l

John Derian
Store: 6 East 2nd Street
New York, NY 10003
+1 212 677 3917
www.johnderian.com
Pages 48a, 130a

**Josephine Macrander,
Interior Decorator**
+31 64 30 53 062
Pages 33al, 105a

picture credits

KEY: *ph*= photographer, **a**=above, **b**=below, **r**=right, **l**=left, **c**=centre.

Endpapers *ph* Polly Wreford/London home of Michael Bains and Catherine Woram; **page 1** *ph* Polly Wreford/Foster House at www.beachstudios.co.uk; **2al** *ph* Claire Richardson/Eifion and Amanda Griffiths of Melin Tregwynt's house in Wales; **2ac** *ph* Polly Wreford/Hilary Robertson and Alistair McGowan, Hastings; **2ar** *ph* Andrew Wood/architect Grethe Meyer's house, Hørsholm, Denmark, built by architects Moldenhawer, Hammer and Frederiksen, 1963; **2cl** *ph* Polly Wreford/Foster House at www.beachstudios.co.uk; **2c** *ph* Chris Tubbs/Hotel Endsleigh; **2cr** *ph* Debi Treloar/Mark and Sally Bailey's home in Herefordshire; **2bl** *ph* Jan Baldwin/art dealer Gul Coskun's apartment in London; **2bc** *ph* Claire Richardson/www.les-sardines.com; **2br** *ph* Catherine Gratwicke/Laura Stoddart's apartment in London; **4** *ph* Polly Wreford/Charlotte-Anne Fidler's home in London; **5** *ph* Debi Treloar/Vine Cottage; **7al** *ph* Debi Treloar/Mark and Sally Bailey's home in Herefordshire; **7ar** *ph* Paul Massey /Jane Packer's home in Suffolk; **7b** *ph* Alan Williams/ceramicist Jette Arendal Winther's home in Denmark, www.arendal-ceramics.com; **8** *ph* Debi Treloar/the guesthouse of the interior designer and artist Philippe Guilmin, Brussels; **9** *ph* Debi Treloar/Mark and Sally Bailey's home in Herefordshire; **10** *ph* Alan Williams/ceramicist Jette Arendal Winther's home in Denmark, www.arendal-ceramics.com; **11** *ph* Christopher Drake/William Yeoward and Colin Orchard's home in London; **12** *ph* Debi Treloar/designer Susanne Rutzou's home in Copenhagen; **13** *ph* Paul Massey/Hôtel Le Sénéchal, Ars en Ré, designed by Christophe Ducharme Architecte; **14–15** *ph* Paul Massey/Jane Packer's home in Suffolk; **16–17** *ph* Debi Treloar/Katrin Arens; **18a** *ph* Debi Treloar/the Philadelphia home of Glen Senk and Keith Johnson of Anthropologie; **18b** *ph* Christopher Drake/Fay and Roger Oates' house in Ledbury; **19al** *ph* Claire Richardson/Nick and Flora Phillips' home in Gascony; **19ar** *ph* Chris Everard/a family home in Norfolk; **19b** *ph* Claire Richardson/Marianne Cotterill's house in London; **20** *ph* Chris Tubbs/designer Emily Todhunter's holiday home in the Peak District; **21** *ph* Debi Treloar/Lucille and Richard Lewin's London house; **22** *ph* Claire Richardson/Eifion and Amanda Griffiths of Melin Tregwynt's house in Wales; **23a** *ph* Catherine Gratwicke/artist Hunt Slonem's own loft in New York; **23bl** *ph* Claire Richardson/Les Trois Salons, Uzes – creators and owners Charmaine and Paul Jack; **23br** *ph* Chris Tubbs/Gabriella Cantaluppi Abbado's home in Monticchiello; **24a** *ph* Claire Richardson/in the London apartment of author and journalist Bradley Quinn; **24b** *ph* Polly Wreford/Foster House at www.beachstudios.co.uk; **25** *ph* Catherine Gratwicke/Martin Barrell and Amanda Sellers' flat, owners of Maisonette, London; **26** *ph* Polly Wreford/Robert Levithan residence, New York City; **27a** *ph* Polly Wreford/Foster House at www.beachstudios.co.uk; **27bl** *ph* Debi Treloar/Catherine Chermayeff and Jonathan David's family home in New York, designed by Asfour Guzy Architects; **27br** *ph* Paul Massey/Michael Giannelli and Greg Shano's home in East Hampton; **28** *ph* Catherine Gratwicke/Laura Stoddart's apartment in London; **29l** *ph* Claire Richardson/Marianne Cotterill's house in London; **29r** *ph* Polly Wreford/Hilary Robertson and Alistair McGowan, Hastings; **30** *ph* Claire Richardson/a family home in Blackheath, South London; **31al** *ph* Polly Wreford/Charlotte-Anne Fidler's home in London; **31ar** *ph* Paul Massey/Naja Lauf; **31bl** *ph* Winfried Heinze/the apartment of Lars Kristensen, owner of Fil de Fer, Copenhagen; **31br** *ph* Polly Wreford/Foster House at www.beachstudios.co.uk; **32** *ph* Lisa Cohen/the home in London of Abigail Ahern, www.atelierabigailahern.com; **33al** *ph* Debi Treloar/Josephine Macrander, interior decorator; **33bl&ar** *ph* Chris Tubbs/Ben Pentreath's Georgian flat in Bloomsbury; **33br** *ph* Catherine Gratwicke/Lulu Guinness's home in London; **34–35** *ph* Polly Wreford; **36al** *ph* Alan Williams/the Norfolk home of Geoff and Gilly Newberry of Bennison Fabrics; **36ar** *ph* Paul Massey/flowers by Jane Packer, location from www.jjlocations.co.uk; **36bl** *ph* Jo Tyler; **36br** *ph* Debi Treloar/author, stylist and Caravan (shop) owner Emily Chalmers and director Chris Richmond's home in London; **37a** *ph* Polly Wreford/photographer Michael Paul's house in London; **37b** *ph* Debi Treloar/Kristiina Ratia and Jeff Gocke's family home in Norwalk, Connecticut; **38al** *ph* Claire Richardson/Swan House Bed and Breakfast in Hastings; **38ar** *ph* Polly Wreford/Emma Greenhill's London home; **38br** *ph* Polly Wreford/Sasha Waddell's home available from www.beachstudios.co.uk; **39** *ph*

Christopher Drake/owners of La Cour Beaudeval Antiquities, Mireille and Jean Claude Lothon's house in Faverolles; **40l** *ph* Debi Treloar/author, stylist and Caravan (shop) owner Emily Chalmers and director Chris Richmond's home in London; **40r** *ph* Debi Treloar/the guesthouse of the interior designer and artist Philippe Guilmin, Brussels; **41l** *ph* Debi Treloar/owner of Crème de la Crème à la Edgar, Helle Høgsbro Krag's home in Copenhagen; **41r** *ph* Debi Treloar/Michael Leva's home in Litchfield County, Connecticut; **42** *ph* Paul Massey/flowers by Jane Packer, location from www.jjlocations.co.uk; **43** *ph* Chris Tubbs/Philip and Catherine Mould's house in Oxfordshire; **44l** *ph* Claire Richardson/available for photographic location at www.inspacelocations.com; **44r** *ph* Polly Wreford/ Emma Greenhill's London home; **45l** *ph* Paul Massey/Hôtel Le Sénéchal, Ars en Ré, designed by Christophe Ducharme Architecte; **45r** *ph* Paul Massey/ the home in Denmark of Charlotte Lynggaard, designer of Ole Lynggaard Copenhagen; **46** *ph* Polly Wreford/Francesca Mills' house in London; **47l** *ph* Christopher Drake/Valentina Albini's home in Milan; **47ar** *ph* Polly Wreford/ Sasha Waddell's home available from www.beachstudios.co.uk; **47br** *ph* Debi Treloar/Anna Massee of Het Grote Avontuur (The Great Adventure)'s home in Amsterdam; **48a** *ph* Debi Treloar/John Derian's apartment in New York; **48bl** *ph* Debi Treloar/Debi Treloar's home in London; **48br** *ph* Claire Richardson/ Marianne Cotterill's house in London; **49l** *ph* Debi Treloar/the guesthouse of the interior designer and artist Philippe Guilmin, Brussels; **49r** *ph* Debi Treloar/Debi Treloar's home in London; **50–51** *ph* Lisa Cohen/the home in London of Abigail Ahern, www.atelierabigailahern.com; **52–53 main** *ph* Debi Treloar/Christina and Allan Thaulow's home in Denmark; **53al&br** *ph* Lisa Cohen/the home of designer Marijke van Nunen; **53ar** *ph* Sandra Lane/Karen Nicol and Peter Clark's home in London; **54a** *ph* Lisa Cohen/Kate Forman's home; **54b** *ph* Claire Richardson/Eifion and Amanda Griffiths of Melin Tregwynt's house in Wales; **55al** *ph* Debi Treloar/available for photographic location at www.inspacelocations.com; **55ar** *ph* Sandra Lane/Robert Elms and Christina Wilson's family home in London; **55b** *ph* Lisa Cohen/the home of designer Marijke van Nunen; **56a** *ph* Debi Treloar/private house in Amsterdam, owner Ank de la Plume; **56bl** *ph* Claire Richardson/Eifion and Amanda Griffiths of Melin Tregwynt's house in Wales; **56–57b** *ph* Claire Richardson/black and white chinaware by Missoni, cushions and tablecloth by Marimekko; **57al&br** *ph* Lisa Cohen/the home of designer Marijke van Nunen; **57ar** *ph* Claire Richardson/ Graham Noakes of Osborne & Little's home in London; **58l** *ph* Lisa Cohen/the home in London of Abigail Ahern, www.atelierabigailahern.com; **58ar** *ph* Chris Tubbs/Raffaella Barker's house in Norfolk; **58br** *ph* Chris Tubbs/Matthew and Miranda Eden's home in Wiltshire; **59** *ph* Lisa Cohen/the designers Piet and Karin Boon's home near Amsterdam, www.pietboon.nl; **60 & 61al** *ph* Lisa Cohen; **61ar** *ph* Sandra Lane; **61b** *ph* Chris Tubbs/the Norfolk home of Geoff and Gilly Newberry of Bennison Fabrics; **62 & 63** *ph* Lisa Cohen/Kate Forman's home; **64a** *ph* Polly Wreford/London home of Michael Bains and Catherine Woram; **64bl** *ph* Sandra Lane/cushions from Charlotte Casadejus; **64br** *ph* Polly Wreford/the Shelter Island home of Lois Draegin and David Cohen; **65** *ph* Polly Wreford/Foster House at www.beachstudios.co.uk; **66a** *ph* Davd Loftus; **66b** *ph* Polly Wreford/Sasha Waddell's home available from www.beachstudios.co.uk; **67al** *ph* Paul Massey/the Bartons' seaside home in West Sussex: www.thedodo.co.uk; **67ac** *ph* Winfried Heinze; **67ar** *ph* Polly Wreford/Sasha Waddell's home available from www.beachstudios.co.uk; **67bl** *ph* Christopher Drake/Florence and Pierre Pallardy, Domaine de la Baronnie, Saint-Martin de Ré; **67br** *ph* Polly Wreford/Foster House at www.beachstudios.co.uk; **68–69** *ph* Claire Richardson/the home of writer Meredith Daneman in London; **70al** *ph* Jan Baldwin/art dealer Gul Coskun's apartment in London; **70bl** *ph* Lisa Cohen; **70br** *ph* Debi Treloar/the home of Netty Nauta in Amsterdam; **71al** *ph* Chris Tubbs/Justin and Eliza Meath Baker's house in the West Country; **71bl** *ph* David Loftus; **71r** *ph* Paul Massey/Jan Constantine – www.janconstantine.com; **72 & 73al** *ph* Christopher Drake/Nordic Style kitchen; **73ar** *ph* David Loftus; **73bl** *ph* Christopher Drake/Valentina Albini's home in Milan; **73br** *ph* Debi Treloar/Annelie Bruijn's home in Amsterdam; **74** *ph* Catherine Gratwicke/Laura Stoddart's apartment in London; **75al** *ph* Andrew Wood/Michael Asplund's apartment in Stockholm, Sweden; **75ar** *ph* Claire Richardson/the home of Fiona and Woody Woodhouse in Herefordshire; **75b & 76l** *ph* Lisa Cohen/the designer Nina Hartmann's home in Sweden, www.vintagebynina.com; **76r** *ph* Debi Treloar/Riad 'Chambres d'Amis' in Marrakech (B&B), designed and owned by Ank de la Plume, decorated in co-production with Household Hardware and Rutger Jan de Lange; **77al** *ph* Polly Wreford/London home of Michael Bains and Catherine

Woram; **77ar** *ph* Debi Treloar/designer Petra Boase and family's home in Norfolk; **77b** *ph* Catherine Gratwicke/artist Hunt Slonem's own loft in New York; **78al** *ph* Catherine Gratwicke/Martin Barrell and Amanda Sellers' flat, owners of Maisonette, London; **78ar** *ph* Debi Treloar/Lucille and Richard Lewin's London house; **78bl** *ph* Polly Wreford/Charlotte-Anne Fidler's home in London; **78br** *ph* Chris Tubbs/Simon and Antonia Johnson's home in Somerset; **79l** *ph* Polly Wreford/Foster House at www.beachstudios.co.uk; **79r** *ph* Polly Wreford; **80l** *ph* Andrew Wood/Ristomatti Ratia's apartment in Helsinki, Finland; **80ar** *ph* Debi Treloar/owner of Crème de la Crème à la Edgar, Helle Høgsbro Krag's home in Copenhagen; **80b** *ph* Paul Massey/Michael Giannelli and Greg Shano's home in East Hampton; **81** *ph* Debi Treloar/the guesthouse of the interior designer and artist Philippe Guilmin, Brussels; **82** *ph* Paul Massey/Michael Giannelli and Greg Shano's home in East Hampton; **83al** *ph* Paul Massey/Jane Packer's home in Suffolk; **83bl** *ph* Chris Tubbs/Diana Sieff's home in Devon; **83r** *ph* Lisa Cohen/the designer Nina Hartmann's home in Sweden, www.vintagebynina.com; **84al** *ph* Chris Tubbs; **84cl** *ph* Alan Williams/Louise Robbins' house in north-west Herefordshire; **84bl** *ph* Debi Treloar/the guesthouse of the interior designer and artist Philippe Guilmin, Brussels; **84r** *ph* Debi Treloar/Katrin Arens; **85** *ph* Chris Tubbs/Annabel Grey's Norfolk cottage; **86–87** *ph* Debi Treloar/Lucille and Richard Lewin's London house; **88a** *ph* Chris Tubbs/Powers house, London; **88b** *ph* Chris Everard/an apartment in Milan designed by Nicoletta Marazza; **88–89** *ph* Andrew Wood/architect Grethe Meyer's house, Hørsholm, Denmark, built by architects Moldenhawer, Hammer and Frederiksen, 1963; **90** *ph* Polly Wreford/Peri Wolfman and Charles Gold's New York loft; **91bl** *ph* Chris Everard/photographer Guy Hills' house in London designed by Joanna Rippon and Maria Speake of Retrouvius; **91ar** *ph* Paul Massey/Jane Packer's home in Suffolk; **91br** *ph* Christopher Drake/owners of French Country Living, the Hill family's home on the Côte d'Azur; **92l** *ph* Lisa Cohen/the home of designer Marijke van Nunen; **92r** *ph* Tom Leighton; **93al** *ph* Polly Wreford/Foster House at www.beachstudios.co.uk; **93ar** *ph* Chris Tubbs/Powers house, London; **93bl** *ph* Debi Treloar/design: Cecilia Proserpio; **93br** *ph* Polly Wreford/Peri Wolfman and Charles Gold's New York loft; **94al** *ph* Debi Treloar/the home of Patty Collister in London, owner of An Angel At My Table; **94bl** *ph* Polly Wreford/Peri Wolfman and Charles Gold's New York loft; **94br** Polly Wreford/Foster House at www.beachstudios.co.uk; **95l** *ph* Debi Treloar/Cristine Tholstrup Hermansen and Helge Drenck's house in Copenhagen; **95r** *ph* Andrew Wood/architect Grethe Meyer's house, Hørsholm, Denmark, built by architects Moldenhawer, Hammer and Frederiksen, 1963; **96al** *ph* Debi Treloar/the London home of Louise Scott-Smith of www.lovelylovely.co.uk; **96bl** *ph* Chris Everard/fashion designer Catherine Malandrino's Manhattan apartment; **96ar** *ph* Debi Treloar/private house in Amsterdam, owner Ank de la Plume; **97** *ph* Claire Richardson/Graham Noakes of Osborne & Little's home in London; **98–99** *ph* Polly Wreford/Kathy Bruml's home in New Jersey; **100a** *ph* Debi Treloar/Annelie Bruijn's home in Amsterdam; **100b** *ph* Debi Treloar/Nikki Tibbles' London home, owner of Wild at Heart – Flowers and Interiors; **101a both** *ph* Debi Treloar/Mark and Sally Bailey's home in Herefordshire; **101b** *ph* Christopher Drake/Fiona and Woody Woodhouse's 16th-century weatherboard cottage in Surrey designed by Bexon Woodhouse Creative; **102a&bl** *ph* Polly Wreford/Foster House at www.beachstudios.co.uk; **102br** *ph* Claire Richardson/Marianne Cotterill's house in London; **103** *ph* Claire Richardson/Eifion and Amanda Griffiths of Melin Tregwynt's house in Wales; **104** *ph* Polly Wreford/Siobhán McKeating's home in London; **105a** *ph* Debi Treloar/Josephine Macrander, interior decorator; **105bl** *ph* Debi Treloar/Clare and David Mannix-Andrews' house, Hove, East Sussex; **105br** *ph* Debi Treloar/Mark and Sally Bailey's home in Herefordshire; **106a** *ph* Chris Tubbs/Powers house, London; **106b** *ph* Chris Tubbs/John Martin Robinson's house in Lancashire; **107** *ph* Sandra Lane/Harriet Scott of R.K. Alliston's apartment in London, throw from Muskett and Muzzullo; **108** *ph* Polly Wreford/Francesca Mills' house in London; **109al** *ph* Debi Treloar/a London apartment designed by James Soane and Christopher Ash of Project Orange; **109bl** *ph* Chris Everard/Yuen-Wei Chew's apartment in London; **109r** *ph* Chris Everard/Davy Hezeman and Steven Pooters' home in Amsterdam; **110l** *ph* Lisa Cohen/the home of Lars Wiberg of Pour Quoi in Copenhagen; **110–111** *ph* Chris Tubbs/Giorgio and Ilaria Miani's Podere Buon Riposo in Val d'Orcia (available to rent); **112** *ph* Polly Wreford/Robert Levithan residence, New York City; **113a** *ph* Winfried Heinze/Polly and Bella's rooms in South London; **113b** *ph* Polly Wreford/Alex Knox; **114l** *ph* Chris Tubbs/Powers house, London; **114ar** *ph* Catherine Gratwicke; **114b** *ph* Debi Treloar/Marcus Hewitt and Susan Hopper's

home in Litchfield County, Connecticut; **115** *ph* Dan Duchars/architect Haifa Hammami's home in London; **116al** *ph* Chris Everard/a house in London designed by Helen Ellery of The Plot London; **116ar** *ph* Jan Baldwin/Mark Smith's home in the Cotswolds; **116bl** *ph* Polly Wreford/Siobhán McKeating's home in London; **116br** *ph* Christopher Drake/antique dealer and co-owner of Jamb Ltd – antique chimneypieces; **117a** *ph* Debi Treloar/Sanne Hjermind and Claes Bech-Poulsen; **117b** *ph* Paul Massey/the home in Denmark of Charlotte Lynggaard, designer of Ole Lynggaard Copenhagen; **118al** *ph* Andrew Wood/Eero Aarnio's house in Veikkola, Finland; **118ar** *ph* Polly Wreford/Siobhán McKeating's home in London; **118b** *ph* Debi Treloar/Roeline Faber, interior designer; **119** *ph* Polly Wreford/Charlotte-Anne Fidler's home in London; **120al** *ph* Christopher Drake/Valentina Albini's home in Milan; **120ar** *ph* Claire Richardson/interior design consultant Rachel van der Brug's home in Amsterdam; **120bl** *ph* Claire Richardson/Eifion and Amanda Griffiths of Melin Tregwynt's house in Wales; **120br** *ph* Debi Treloar/the London home of Sam Robinson, co-owner of The Cross and Cross the Road; **121l** *ph* Chris Tubbs/Julia and Michael Pruskin's family home; **121r** *ph* Claire Richardson/Marianne Cotterill's house in London; **122–123** *ph* Debi Treloar/designer Susanne Rutzou's home in Copenhagen; **124a** *ph* Claire Richardson/the London townhouse belonging to Louise Laycock of Bennison; **124bl** *ph* Catherine Gratwicke; **124br** *ph* Chris Tubbs/Annabel Grey's Norfolk cottage; **125** *ph* Polly Wreford/Ben de Lisi's home in London; **126** *ph* Debi Treloar/Mark and Sally Bailey's home in Herefordshire; **127a** *ph* Debi Treloar/the Chestnut Hill home of Pamela Falk; **127bl** *ph* Chris Tubbs/Elizabeth Baer's early Georgian home; **127br** *ph* Chris Tubbs/Justin and Eliza Meath Baker's house in the West Country; **128** *ph* Lisa Cohen/Anna McDougall's London home; **129a** *ph* Debi Treloar/Sanne Hjermind and Claes Bech-Poulsen; **129bl&br** *ph* Debi Treloar/Mark and Sally Bailey's home in Herefordshire; **130a** *ph* Debi Treloar/John Derian's apartment in New York; **130bl** *ph* Polly Wreford/Robert Levithan Residence, New York City; **130br** *ph* Christopher Drake/owners of La Cour Beaudeval Antiquities, Mireille and Jean Claude Lothon's house in Faverolles; **131** *ph* Chris Tubbs/Elizabeth Baer's early Georgian home; **132** *ph* Chris Tubbs/Annabel Grey's Norfolk cottage; **133a** *ph* Paul Massey/Michael Giannelli and Greg Shano's home in East Hampton; **133bl** *ph* Catherine Gratwicke/gallery and bookshop owner Françoise de Nobele's apartment in Paris; **133br** *ph* Christopher Drake/Maurizio Epifani's home in Milan; **134l** *ph* Debi Treloar/the home of Joanne Cleasby, Hove; **134ar** *ph* Debi Treloar/Annelie Bruijn's home in Amsterdam; **134br** *ph* Debi Treloar/Mark and Sally Bailey's home in Herefordshire; **135** *ph* Christopher Drake/textile designer Neisha Crosland's London home; **136–137** *ph* Chris Tubbs/Annabel Grey's Norfolk cottage; **138a** *ph* Claire Richardson/the home of Fiona and Woody Woodhouse in Herefordshire; **138b** *ph* Claire Richardson; **138–139** *ph* Chris Tubbs; **140** *ph* Claire Richardson/www.chambres-provence.com; **141a** *ph* Chris Everard/Manhattan home of designer Matthew Patrick Smyth; **141b** *ph* Christopher Drake/William Yeoward and Colin Orchard's home in London; **142l** *ph* Claire Richardson/the home of Charmaine and Paul Jack – Belvezet, France; **142r** *ph* Paul Massey/Cote Jardin boutique; **143** *ph* Paul Massey/Jan Constantine – www.janconstantine.com; **144** *ph* Polly Wreford/Hilary Robertson and Alistair McGowan, Hastings; **145al** *ph* Catherine Gratwicke/interior designer Sue West's house in Gloucestershire; **145ar** *ph* Chris Tubbs/Gabriella Cantaluppi Abbado's home in Monticchiello; **145b** *ph* Debi Treloar/owners of Maisonette, Martin Barrell and Amanda Sellers' home in London; **146** *ph* Debi Treloar/www.juliaclancey.com; **147al** *ph* Debi Treloar/Mark and Sally Bailey's home in Herefordshire; **147ar** *ph* Winfried Heinze/Stella's room in New York City; **147b** *ph* Debi Treloar/www.juliaclancey.com; **148a** *ph* Paul Massey/Jane Packer's home in Suffolk; **148b** *ph* Chris Tubbs/Diana Sieff's home in Devon; **149al** *ph* Paul Ryan/the home of Nils Tunebjer in Sweden; **149cl** *ph* Polly Wreford/Harriet Maxwell Macdonald's home in London; **149bl** *ph* Polly Wreford/London home of Michael Bains and Catherine Woram; **149ar** *ph* Polly Wreford/Foster House at www.beachstudios.co.uk; **149br** *ph* Paul Massey/the Bartons' seaside home in West Sussex: www.thedodo.co.uk; **150** *ph* Paul Massey; **151al** *ph* Paul Massey/Cote Jardin boutique; **151ar** *ph* Paul Massey/Hotel Tresanton, St Mawes, Cornwall, owned and designed by Olga Polizzi; **151br** *ph* Caroline Arber/Caroline Zoob; **152a** *ph* Christopher Drake/Maurizio Epifani's home in Milan; **152bl** *ph* Winfried Heinze/Josephine Ryan's house in London; **152br** *ph* Winfried Heinze/a family home in Brighton; **153** *ph* Chris Tubbs/Justin and Eliza Meath Baker's house in the West Country; **160** *ph* Polly Wreford/Foster House at www.beachstudios.co.uk.

acknowledgments

Writing a book is never easy, but the process is always less difficult if you have the perfect, enthusiastic team making everything run like clockwork. So, thank you so much Alison Starling and Leslie Harrington, and Clare Double and Toni Kay; and a particular thank you to Emily Westlake, whose inspired idea it was in the first place!